Forward

We are all born naked—vulnerable—into a room often too cold, too bright, from a womb that was temperature-controlled and nourishing and safe. We are here and we are now. Time and space mean nothing. Even the idea of "meaning" means nothing.

But we are thrown into a rushing river of objects and images that demand who, how, why, when, what, where. From that rushing river emerges a curious something – ME.

From these pages I leap out at you as you get to meet me still birthing myself.

Welcome.

ARTIST'S PRAYER

To the universal light within all of us,

Remind me of your authorship.
Open my eyes so that I can see your open doors.
Give me the courage to do what's right for me.
Inspire me to be audacious—to put it out there.
Let it all be enhanced by your love . . .
And your joy.

Thank you,

Mark

MOOD ONE

What days were those, in New York autumn cold?
When a lonely chill took measured steps along your body,

And windows away you saw an ancient sun.
From your perch you viewed an empty street.
You felt somehow akin to the rolling crackling leaves,

Now and then jumping, rushing in the whisper
Of the reckless meandering wind . . .
After warm dinners and goodnights,
And the before-sleep listening;

It was dark, then, and only the wind spoke to you,
Of giant trees and shrouded playgrounds and
Snows to come. The world darkened
And then you slept.

Introduction

I have been a psychotherapist for the better part of my life, presenting myself as therapist for the first time at the age of seventeen, performing unrequested therapy on my girlfriend's dysfunctional parents. Since that time, I have been enthusiastically plowing through fields of neurosis and reckless communication with unrelenting zeal.

To write a memoir is to stare into a mirror looking for meaning, for direction, and for intention. What does my life mean? How do I feel about my life? What are the forces that drove me in such a wide variety of directions? At what points in time was I in tune with my spiritual direction and what other times was I afloat and out of touch? When was I mindful and when was I mindless? Finding the answers to these questions was often painful. I had learned early in life that the doorway to personal growth is blocked by the fear of embarrassment.

Ever since my conception, music has been a pivotal part of my life—one of profound importance. My father, Sid Weiss, was a world-class jazz bass player, and I grew up in an apartment building in Queens that was bustling with musicians.

In this memoir, I have attempted to look clearly at the moments I chose for truth and at the moments I was simply avoiding fear. Interspersed, there are moments of hilarity and aliveness, depression and despair. I have gathered about me notes, photographs, and videotapes, all with the purpose of awakening the sense of my Self—struggling for leadership of my life despite the various deceivers, seducers, and fear-mongers I've encountered from birth until now. They have forced me to step back, to find the quiet place within me that gives direction and meaning to my actions.

I ask that you offer me the same compassion regarding my life as I have had to learn to give to myself. I invite you to be a worthy witness to the adventures and misadventures, the wins and losses, and the painful buffeting that life brings when you follow your passions.

As I move through my eighth decade, I find myself viewing the world and all of its inhabitants as creatures who are involved in an awakening. It is a sometimes slow, sometimes fast, realization of a larger conscious awareness. To me, awakenings appear to be in two forms: gentle and rude. My life seems to be comprised of many rude awakenings, sort of like the equivalent of cosmic speed-dating.

Many years ago—sometime around 1961, when I was twenty years old—I faced a near-death experience. I decided right then that I had passed the point of enough—the point when I said to myself, "I've had a full, rich life, and although there are lots of things I'd like to do, I've done enough."

It was a post–bucket-list moment; a juncture in my life from which, with pitch-perfect fanfare, my life was relegated to everyone else's memories of me.

I've had such a good and intense time on this planet. I hope you enjoy hearing my stories and songs and looking through my eyes.

NEW YORK

Spiritual Awakening

Bright Moment: My first recognition of spirituality happened at the tender age of five. At the time, I was living in a sixth-floor apartment in Queens. On this particularly fateful night, I was lying in my bunk bed with my brother while my parents played cards downstairs with their friends. As I lay awake in bed, something inside of me made me get up. Some intangible force moved me out of my bedroom onto the balcony. I looked out into the horizon, examining the New York skyline, and as I looked up into the night sky, I beheld the most beautiful array of diamond-like stars imaginable.

Without any thought, I took off my pajamas and stood there, naked on the balcony, just looking—communing—with the cosmos. Even though I had no words for what was going on, I felt totally and utterly connected to the galaxy. It was a very powerful moment in my life.

In all my years, this experience has never left me. It gave me assurance that I was here for a reason and that it was completely appropriate to feel a sense of awe in the cosmos. I never told my parents—or anyone else—of this experience. It was one of those times when being alone was not frightening but rather confirming. I knew that I was on a ride to somewhere, but it really didn't matter where I was going. The only thing that mattered was the ride.

❧

The power of this image stays with me to this day, as does my appreciation for being naked. I have had countless naked experiences with women—naked on balconies, naked in elevators, naked in churches, naked on Indian mounds, naked in the woods, naked in rivers—sometimes chemically enhanced. One of the highlights of this theme for me was the wide array of many naked nights spent in my Atlanta office. On the twenty-ninth floor of Tower Place with enormous glass windows overlooking all of northwest Atlanta, I could often be found—high above the chaos of the world and naked as a jaybird—frolicking in sensual delight.

Later in life, I moved to Memphis and found myself once more on the sixth-floor balcony of an apartment building, frolicking. I was able to be naked and free yet again, knowing that nobody was going to look up from the street. Many of the women that I've loved have delighted in sharing the adventure and riskiness of my balcony trysts. No matter how damaged my body may have appeared to be to me, when I was having these experiences, all limitations ceased to exist.

It took me a long time to make the connection between my sexuality and my spirituality. With each advancing year, I see the Spirit in everyone I love and—hopefully—with everyone I meet. What was at first the joy of wild abandon shifted focus to the blessing of connectedness.

Luckily, the joy of wild abandon is a thread that still travels with me. It has morphed into a fearless kind of Universal joy.

I Wonder if There's Something Wrong with Him?

How easy could it be? I was born in New York City on March 18, 1941. I was a "metal head"—a term I use for a baby who required the use of forceps during birth—but nevertheless, my arrival was about as tranquil as they come. I was my parents' first child, and my delivery only took an hour.

❧ ⁂ ☙

Bright Moment: Right from the start, I was placid, comfortable, and at peace with the world. I was serenely curious about everything. As an infant, people often thought that there was something wrong with me. They thought that I was overly placid and peaceful. I got the best of my mom at that point.

❧ ⁂ ☙

Within hours of my father's discovery that he was a daddy, he was on the Artie Shaw Band bus, drinking and celebrating his daddy-hood. The guys were playing one of those high school boy games where one guy would hit the other guy's arm, and . . . Oops! My dad ended up breaking his wrist—the very same wrist that had taken him to the top as a jazz bass player. Talk about stealing my thunder! Ah, well . . . Luckily, my father found the finest hand surgeon in New York and had his wrist expertly repaired. It was as good as new.

Eight days after my arrival, the family gathered for my bris, and then my father spotted the dirt on the hands of the mohel, a Jew trained in the practice of brit milah, the "covenant of circumcision." In an instant rage, my father threw the mohel out of the operating room and asked for a surgeon.

From the day I was born until the day I left the hospital I managed to set some sort of record for gaining weight. Then, my mother was given a drug to dry up her breast milk. In moments of rumination throughout my life, I often wondered if my extraordinary interest—dare I say, my fixation—on breasts, boobies, milk machines, jugs, knockers, honkers, hooters, frost detectors, Winnebagos, ad infinitum, was related to this fact. I am sure it has, at the very least, influenced my motivation, if not my life direction.

My Father—Seymore "Sid" Weiss

Round head, brush-like short, black hair, well-trimmed mustache, hairy skin. He wore round metal spectacles. He was wiry, medium height—less than six feet tall. He had gotten out of the army and was an impeccable dresser. He had a stiff, upright posture. He was intense. He was passionate about world affairs. Somewhere between a socialist and a communist. He played with Pete Seeger and the Weavers as well as Paul Robeson and attended political meetings. Since the beginning of his career as a jazz bass player in New York, he developed strong relationships with musicians of color and was well respected in the music community.

He was a confirmed pacifist and was committed to not using corporal punishment with me and my brother Gene. I remember his eyes when he was angry.

I didn't detect a sense of emotional connection even though I looked for it. I experienced a shocking iciness.

HI DAD. HAPPY BIRTHDAY.

Hi Dad. Happy birthday.
    I am writing from a great emotional distance
            Full circle again
        My me-ness (meanness) offends you
Start again:
    Hi Dad. Happy birthday.
            Everything I thought I got from you
                I got despite you
Start again:
    Hi Dad. Happy birthday.
            You said, beaming, "You have a pretty wife
                A new car, a nice office, a nice house
                    A nice practice - now if you would
                        Just lose some weight."
Start again:
Hi Dad. Happy birthday.
            This is farewell, isn't it?
                I can't burn my gift for you anymore
Don't start again:

My Mother—Ethel Mae Breeskin Weiss

Mom's full name was Ethel Mae Weiss. Throughout her life, she was Mae to her family and Ethel at work. She was born on Christmas Day in Washington D.C. Her father was a violinist of Russian descent and a classical conductor. He conducted a small orchestra that performed music he selected to be played behind silent movies. He was beloved and admired and an excellent chess player.

My mother was the second born of five children, all the rest of whom were boys. Jackie, the youngest brother, was intellectually disabled but still highly functioning. Barney was the first born, a pianist, and music director at the Shoreham Hotel in Washington D.C., frequented by senators and congressmen. Notably, he knew the favorite song of every famous person that came into the hotel. My mother became the musical booking agent for the Shoreham Hotel.

My grandmother on the other hand was what they called a 'zaftig baleboste': a fully-rounded, in-charge, homemaker who made sure you didn't forget that fact.

My mother described to me a situation in which her own mother found out that her father was having an affair and vividly remembers a scene in which my grandmother was holding my mother in front of her as a shield while she was berating grandpa. Mom said she was frozen; that scene was imprinted on her for life.

Here was my grandfather, a very attractive and sophisticated musician, conductor, who dressed really well, never overweight, a chess player, and then my grandmother, a heavyset, cheerful, sweet, village woman.

When my grandparents left Washington D.C. as most Jews do, they went to Florida, where my grandfather organized and conducted the Miami Beach Symphony Orchestra, and my uncles set him up with a dry-cleaning store to make some money. His successor in the business was Barney. My mother and my Uncle Barney were the only ones that knew that my grandpa really liked the ladies, and they purposely kept that from the three younger brothers, so to the younger brothers, my grandfather was a saint.

Mom. Soft and gentle. Warm and humorous. She was nearly as tall as my father. Not overly affectionate. Round face, soft eyes, soft smile. Hair just past her shoulders, black. She wore her hair down. Her eyes were brown. She smiled and laughed a lot. Her voice was lilting. She dressed mostly conservatively. She would rarely wear anything revealing. At home, she always wore a full dress. She liked bright colors. She loved to read. When she was on the road with my father while the other band wives were playing canasta or poker, my mother would be sitting in the corner reading a book. Often, she read to me.

When I was age three, she rented the ground floor apartment in our six-story building and opened up a kindergarten, preparing kids for going to school.

She planned and conducted occasional religious ceremonies and headed up all parties; decorating and making sure we were honored and acknowledged around birthdays. She often birthed magic.

MIRACLE NAILS

In her eighty-fifth year
My mother's nails sprang from her hands
　　　more beautiful and strong
　　　　　than ever before
Pink. I never saw pink nails
Working hands, washing, typing
　　　the function and the form were one
And now, as if a teenage dream
　　　of perfect nails,
　　　　　pale and pointed,
　　　　　　tapping the tap

                              of strength,
            were humming in her mind's
                   physiology, looking in her body
                          for a plausible reason
Is four score and five
                   a trigger of her body clock
Or the sinking of peace
                   deep into her bones
                          and a fourteen-year-old girl
                                 making the dream come true

∽ ༷ ∾

My Brother—Eugene (Gene) Breeskin Weiss

Gene was a year and a half younger than I. He was born
in a time of social chaos. Our father, a pacifist, found a way to
support the war effort through music while still honoring his
pacifist beliefs. He played in the U.S.O. band which kept him away
from home. That was actually a more peaceful time at home.
However, the climate and reality of wartime took its toll on Gene
over time.

I, CHILD OF WAR

My brother turning twenty-one
            is one
                   born out of war
                          one of many;
Sperm of frightened, hopeful
            boys, trying to erase
                   from their eyes

dead and dying men.
What an inheritance for my
    war-baby brother:
        another war, an old argument,
            Hitler was an anti-communist
Germany's war-babies died for false love
    and now all war-babies
        nearly old enough to love
            are being swallowed up
                by history's grinning mouth
The fiery ones at Berkeley,
    in Mississippi, and all points
    South, are crying;
        they love too much.
        they have met the wondering
            eyes of poverty's children
        and cried at night
            I have cried with them.
These will not argue with dead tongues
    and salute inevitable death
        for cheap medals
Freedom is an early morning cry
    for honest love
        and rights are not for paper dolls
            they are for men.
You, the unloved, strong-willed children
    of war, fed on television's cereals
        and electronic love;
            adjusted, educated on white
                blackboards, saluting
                    a sterile flag of lies
What of you?

Is all you are to learn of life
to be found in machine-gun
jungles, killing another man's
color, slanted eyes, for medals
like stuttering
John Wayne
movies?
Your dances, songs and living heroes
long-haired for want of love
(and you give love to them)
cry "Look at me!"
"I am your forgotten
son or daughter.
I want my own."
This world is yours!
old men, rattling swords,
stand aside! Politicians,
you grasping deadly grandmothers
get out of the way!
We will
not hear your lies.
Love is painful and our world
changes, young trees have you planted
and these will not be destroyed
for yesterday's dreams.
You have taught us, in hospital colleges
to love money and buy marriage
and close our ears to the quiet
sobbing of starvation in our land.

You have taught us fear and empty bravery
"Better dead than red" is an old

Woman's chant of fear.
We are not afraid!
we will face this world and not
destroy it.
We shall overcome!

❧ ⚜ ❧

My mother would say that my brother came running out of the womb. Today he would have been diagnosed as ADHD, Attention Deficit Hyperactivity Disordered. He was hard to manage, and rambunctious. As a child, Gene was shorter than I was with a small, narrow face with dark mischievous eyes and short, dark hair. We had a very caring and supportive relationship.

As the eldest child, I often looked after him. He would hold my hand and look up to me expectantly. I loved being his big brother.

We were unprepared for the tumultuous upheavals of our teenage years. I took the 'good boy' role and he was left with the 'bad boy' role. We were pitted against each other. When he would get in trouble, my mother would refer to it as, "he's going through a phase." That seemed to be the best she could do while dealing with my father's predictably unpredictable anger.

One summer, my father took a job as a bass player with the band at a lodge in upstate New York. He took my brother and me fishing on Schroon Lake. My brother was the only one that caught a fish. We kept it in a pail of water and brought it back to our room. My father decided he was going to cook the fish, and when my brother realized he couldn't take it home as a pet, he began to cry uncontrollably. By the time he got to eat the fish, he had calmed down.

New Rules

Soon after my arrival, the U.S. was entering into World War II, and my father had joined the USO, traveling with the troops, playing with Hal Macintyre's band. My first conscious memory of my dad was of him coming home after the war was over. I was four.

I still remember dad's cigarette smell and the strange khaki of his uniform, his hat, and his huge duffel bag. He was an entirely new person to me. I still have no recollections of him before he left, and yet then I felt obligated to behave as the welcoming firstborn. I tried to help him with his duffel bag.

He brought small gifts without context. The manner in which he presented them seemed almost mechanical. I immediately tensed up and retreated to my mother's side. I heard his words as he asked me questions I didn't know how to answer.

"How old are you?"

"What's your favorite toy?"

"Have you been a good boy?"

Questions that seemed more like interrogations coming from a preoccupied mind.

A whole new set of rules was imposed immediately. My brother and I were told to not make noise before eleven o'clock in the morning, a part of the musician's life we had never experienced before. We were not to touch the record player. Don't touch any of his things. I felt restricted from experiencing any of the things that represented him, and therefore from ever really knowing him.

From the beginning of our relationship, I felt estranged. A chill that never warmed up. Suddenly the sense of being safe and comfortable in my own apartment dropped away and was replaced by a general sense of dread.

Make no noise when Dad was practicing his bass. We weren't allowed to be anywhere around when he was practicing. If we broke his rules, we were bombarded with shaming, rhetorical questions, like, "Don't you realize…?" His tone conveyed a hot controlling anger, masked by rationality. Compressed tightness. He was committed, as was my mother, to not spanking, as he was a committed pacifist, but the effect of his shaming was boiling hot.

My father, when asked for help, would immediately become critical. When I would make normal kid noises in the house before eleven o'clock, he would take it as disrespect and attack me for being inconsiderate. His attacks ranged from tight-lipped accusations to yelling at full volume. He would tell me that I was inconsiderate and occasionally corner me. In my fear, I would freeze, knowing I couldn't explain that it was unintentional.

I was too young to see that this was his poor attempt at child-rearing. In that day, about sixty percent of the adult male population had had the same training.

I felt rebuffed and separate. I genuinely felt disconnected, unable to be heard or understood. It wasn't the words; it was the distant demeanor and high-voltage tone.

⁓ঞ⁓

BRIGHT MOMENT: There was a dream that came to me occasionally, or perhaps it really happened, I'm not sure, in which my mom, dad, and I were in the park in the sunlight. My father had taken off his shirt and was lying in the sun. I saw myself as about one year old, because I was crawling and I was climbing up the mountain of his chest. In that sunlight moment, feeling my father's breath, I felt safe.

❦

My mother provided me with encouraging and comforting support. She was my cheerleader. When I was having difficulty with math homework, from elementary school all the way through high school, Mom provided a mix of directive guidance and support. Her style was to encourage me to solve the problems using small examples, and she took delight in my successes.

The dynamics of my family life had shifted from the warm, intelligent care of my mother to the distant and often fearful environment my father provided. He was self-absorbed, focusing on his bass practice at home and his work at NBC Studios. He was playing on several well-known radio and TV shows, such as The Frances Langford-Don Ameche Show and The Arthur Godfrey Show. I remember going into the city to see the shows and to hear him play once.

One of the most positive and nourishing images I have with my father was going to Carnegie Hall to hear Beethoven's Fifth Symphony conducted by Toscanini. I was transfixed. The attitude of the audience was worshipful, and I was touched by it. Even in that circumstance, I felt like I was sitting next to a stranger. There was no meaningful sharing of feelings or observations, so even with a beautiful moment in time like that, I felt alone.

The atmosphere of our family was impacted most deeply by an angry and jealous energy my father projected onto us. He felt that our lives were so much easier than his. In his family of origin, they only spoke Yiddish until he began school. This made his school entry like that of a foreign student, even though he wasn't. His mother died when he was seven years old and he was passed from house to house until his father remarried. He carried that unhealed wound in which he was the victim around with him and unleashed it on Gene and me.

It seemed strange to me that when other kids came over to my house to visit, they thought my father was friendly, warm, and engaging. When they would tell me how jealous they were that he was so cool, I was mystified. I felt like they had come to the wrong house. He was that way with everyone outside of our family.

Another outcome of the impact of my father's anger was what I came to call "The Small War" between my mother and father. I would see my father being mean to my mother. I don't think I quite understood the full dynamic, but I could see her hurting, her frustration, and often her feelings of loneliness. It was as if I would get on my little white pony and go racing up the hill to rescue her and she would be in bed with a dragon.

Rarely was there arguing between my parents in the presence of my brother or me. Years later, as I understood the dynamics of family systems, I recognized some patterns. My mother's strategy in the face of my father's bullying would be to appear compliant on the surface while harboring resentments. She would withdraw from my father in the face of his anger and put on eighty pounds—which would infuriate my father—and then, as things cooled down, she would struggle to lose the weight.

Once again, my father would explode and push her away and the feedback loop would continue over and over.

This cycle affected my brother and me by making us hypervigilant. As with many children, we had a psychic awareness of what was going on, although we wouldn't have been able to express it.

Every night when he would come home from the Johnny Carson show, he brought jokes home with him. During each television show, the band, after introducing the show, would sit around backstage and tell jokes, and my father would tell those jokes to my brother, mother and me the next day. I thought they were hilarious, and many years later came to realize that the majority of the jokes were what I call dope jokes or hipster humor.

⌘

"Two hipsters are standing in front of a movie theater gettin' high smoking dope. A set of identical twins comes out of the theater and go in opposite directions. One hipster says to the other, "How did he do that?"

"Two hipsters are standing on the street corner smoking dope and a motorcycle speeds by at eighty miles per hour. One hipster says to the other, "I thought he'd never leave."

⌘

In spite of his abuse, the more I admired him, the more I wanted him to love me. I believe that where there is contact between father and son, there is often the transmission of a moral imperative, a message the father hands to the son, who swallows it whole in the effort to be loved. Mine was "You should make a contribution to the world."

This may have come from his Jewish background. It certainly was related to his activities among socialists in New York, and I carried it like a badge. This was my assignment. At the age of thirteen, my goal was to work for the United Nations doing conflict resolution, so many of the activities that dominated my life were generated from that one thought. I'm still waiting for that call from the United Nations.

My father was at the top of the DownBeat Poll. This was a yearly list in an American magazine devoted to music performance. He was in the category for "jazz, blues, and beyond." He was in the number one spot for years as the best jazz bass player, but he never practiced jazz nor listened to jazz recordings at home. He only practiced classical music. I was excluded from any conversation about and exposure to his real music.

He studied classical bass with one of the best teachers in New York: Milt Kestenbaum. Milt was the first adult male I made contact with at age seven or eight who spoke to me as if I were an adult. He had a wonderful, warm sense of humor and showed genuine interest in how my life was going.

My experience with him—although brief—put my relationship with my father in silhouette. I began to recognize the absence of a genuine connection with my father. As is typical with kids, my brother and I still vied for his attention and an authentic bond. Much of the competition that arose between Gene and I was due to the fact that we were adversaries in the fight to get my father's very occasional attention.

Years later, as I began to understand the dynamics of my relationship with Gene, I could see how at some point it had shifted from one of caring to one of angry competition. One of my few regrets is that I was never able to repair the relationship with Gene, as his premature death at the age of 36 in a boating accident ended that possibility.

Growing up in my household, there was never a dull moment. My parents were out-and-out New York Jewish socialists. We were called red-diaper babies—children of Communists. Being born to doctrinaire socialists in New York City exposed me to a variety of emotional and intellectual connections to the African American community. My father played bass with Benny Goodman and Artie Shaw, both of whom were musical pioneers in breaking the color barrier. Dad also played with Paul Robeson and with Pete Seeger and the Weavers, and he was there on the scene for the Peekskill Riots.

Before she married my father, my mother was the president of the Jazz Society of Washington, D.C. with two years of college behind her.

I was completely surrounded by talented musicians and singers throughout my early childhood. I looked on as my parents had friends at our apartment in Queens who were at the height of their careers—Billie Holiday, Buck Clayton, Peggy Lee, and many others. At the time of my mother's first pregnancy, Billie Holiday wanted to be my godmother. I am relying heavily on the stories my mother told me, since most of these events occurred before I had any conscious memory.

What I can still remember are the summer mornings, being awakened by a tenor sax player running scales on the fire escape, beautifully contrasted against the racket of the elevated subway and the kids playing stickball in the street. During my early years, we lived up on the top floor of a six-story apartment building on Whitney Avenue in Queens. I could see the skyline of New York, the view faded as hundreds of six-story buildings crept toward the sky. We were close enough to LaGuardia airport that we could actually see faces in the cockpits of the planes as they soared over our roof.

PS 89

In my family, we had a long-standing tradition of engaging in social action. My father was involved with a lot of labor union groups. He was among the musicians that broke the color barrier by playing with band leaders like Benny Goodman and Artie Shaw who hired black musicians and had to fight racist resistance because of it.

When I was around eight years old, my parents sent my brother and me to an extraordinary camp in the mountains. It was my first intentionally racially integrated experience, and I loved it. We learned freedom songs and folk songs, and we painted and shared. People like Pete Seeger, Joan Baez, Woody Guthrie, and Joni Mitchell performed for us at the camp and taught us quite an array of progressive songs.

The lyrics to one of the songs we learned there have always stayed with me:

"I went down to the St. James Infirmary, and I saw some plasma there, so I ups and asks the doctor man, was the donor dark or fair? The doctor put down his reading book, and he gave me a very scientific look, and he said a corpuscle is a corpuscle, and the damn thing's got no race."

We were surrounded at this camp by people who came from a humanistic background and had all the right values for a socialist family. Shortly after our time at the camp, Senator Joe McCarthy began his attack on liberals, socialists, and communists. The communists were referred to as the Reds, so if you were not a full-blooded communist but still had those leanings, they called you a Pinko. My father belonged to some organizations that were deemed communist by the government and felt he might be targeted.

My parents were so frightened that they were going to be called up before the Senate committee that they incinerated all the progressive books in their house. They were terrified. It took my father many years before he would apply for any Civil Service job that required FBI screening.

My mother had also been a pioneer in the field of social activism. She was the president of the PTA, and she had arranged to bring a famous New York dance troupe to our school to perform. The name of my school was Public School 89, better known as PS 89, in Queens, New York.

Katherine Dunham was the leader of the dance troupe. She was quite famous at the time, and she and all of the other members of the dance troupe were black. My mother had left that little bit of information out when she spoke with the principal of the school to set up the performance. The principal and several other PTA members were waiting at the curb along with my mother as a huge bus pulled up in front of them. When the doors of the bus opened, out stepped these beautiful, muscular, athletic black dancers. The principal nearly had a heart attack! PS 89 was an all-white school at the time.

After the performance, much to my mother's dismay, she couldn't find a restaurant anywhere in our neighborhood that would serve an all-black dance troupe, so she prepared the food herself and squeezed everyone from the dance troupe into our two-bedroom apartment. Years later, when my mother would tell the story of that day, there was always a twinkle in her eye. She always did enjoy fighting for a good cause.

She had also been instrumental in bringing the first black teacher into our school, along with her two children—the first two black students to ever attend PS 89.

My own first personal experience with social action wouldn't take place until a few years later. Although I had moved on to junior high school at that point, I came back to PS 89 one afternoon to visit some friends. I was on the playground when I saw a number of white kids chasing two black kids. As if the fact that they were chasing and bullying them wasn't bad enough, to make matters worse, they were calling these kids some vicious racial slurs. Something began to well up inside of me—an overwhelming indignation. At that moment, I was overcome by rage, and I grabbed both of the white kids by the scruff of their necks, then smashed their heads together.

"You can't do this!" I screamed at them.

I was furious. I don't know what exactly it was that came over me that day, but it felt like I had to do something to stop it. This act required no thought on my part. I had been suddenly triggered into action. Then, just as quickly as it had started, everything inside of me became distinctly quiet again once it was over. This was an inner experience that would repeat throughout my life.

Aside from the utter indignation at racially motivated bullying and prejudice, I had been pretty easygoing. For six years—which was basically my entire stint at PS 89—I'd harbored a major crush on Helena Wolf. She was the same height as I was, and her last name started with 'W', so whether the class was organized alphabetically or by height, we would always end up next to each other.

In the first grade, Helena and I had been asked by our teacher to look after a young French boy, Alain, who was new to our country. This was a task that we took very seriously, and with genuine care we made every effort to make him feel comfortable. After that, we stayed pretty close throughout elementary school.

When the time came for me to graduate from the sixth grade, I was speaking with a friend of mine named Warren about what sort of plans we could make to celebrate. We decided that he would ask his girlfriend—and I would ask Helena—to go with us into New York City. It had not once occurred to me that I needed to ask my mother for permission. Warren and I had planned and scheduled for the big day, and Helena was ready for me to arrive to take her to the Empire State Building by subway. Just as I was heading out the door on my way to pick her up, my mother stopped me and asked where I was going. I explained to her the plans that Warren and I had made for the day. To my shock and utter dismay, she shut it all down with two simple words: "Absolutely no!"

I felt so much shame at disappointing Helena that I couldn't even bring myself to call her, so I asked Warren to do so instead. That day remained embedded in my mind for many years to come, and later in life when I was facing a near-death experience, I decided to write a letter addressed to Helena Wolf—

a letter with no address. In the letter, I apologized sincerely for that day. I was glad to finally find some relief by forgiving myself.

At the same time as this event with Helena took place, I was selected to be a part of a special progress program at a junior high school, PS 16 in Corona, New York, and I never returned again to PS 89.

PS 16

After leaving PS 89, I went on to attend seventh grade junior high school at PS 16 in Corona—a crowded neighborhood in the New York City borough of Queens. The special progress program I was in allowed students to complete three years of work in only two years. It was obvious to see that I was one of the youngest, least mature, and most naive of the kids in the program. This was the first time I had been away from home and away from my friends, but I was doing my best to adjust to all the changes.

Approximately half of the student body there was African American while the other half was Italian. To most of the Italian students, Jews were nothing more than "Christ killers" and within the first few days of attending school there, I'd already formed my first alliances with black students, where I had found not only friends, but also a certain degree of protection.

One thing I will always remember about this school was that every year, there was a a gang war between the black students and the Italian students. They would defoliate the trees in the park next to our school by tearing branches off of them and attacking the other side. This all happened around the same time as the release of the movie The Blackboard Jungle, which depicted racial and religious battles in high school. Racial tensions were extremely high pretty much everywhere, and PS 16 was no exception.

I was completely unprepared emotionally for the accelerated academic program, and I had difficulty keeping up my grades. This led me to perform my first act of deception by signing my own report cards instead of letting my parents see them, which was a very short-term solution. Of course, I ended up getting caught, and my parents and I had to come up to the school for a meeting. I promised that I would never do it again, and they bought it, but I had become so unhappy in the program at that point that I began to take other drastic measures. I decided on my own that I was going to quit the special progress class.

After my mind was made up, instead of attending the advanced class, I wandered down to the band room in the basement and asked the teacher, Mr. Fink, if I could join the band. He did not question me about my class status or obligations. He simply said that it was fine with him, and his only question for me was, which instrument I would like to play? Clarinets and saxophones seemed horribly complex to me. Trumpets, on the other hand, appeared to have only three notes, and I was drawn to their simplicity. Mr. Fink led me into another room and showed me how to play an 'F' on the trumpet, and after that, I was off and running. Once I learned more about music and was ensconced in the band, I even volunteered to be the bass player for a little band that Mr. Fink had formed.

My father had taken notice of my interest in music and came to the conclusion that he should be my bass teacher. What an enormous mistake that was! His perfectionism and shaming were so intense that within one short year, I had accidently broken the necks of three different basses—one of which was my father's practice bass.

For many years after that experience, after switching to trombone, when reading music, I remained unable to play a high note without closing my eyes in anxiety and fear of missing the note. This was not a good idea for a musician and often, that anxiety caused me to miss the note. Years later I learned this was called an "aw, shit" note. Needless to say, I was impaired for quite some time by the angst and pressure brought on by having my father as a music teacher for about a year of pure hell.

Also, around that same time, I was approaching the day of my birthday bar mitzvah. As the first grandchild in our family, this was important. I should point out that I am a faux Jew. I like some of the music, but I don't like the rules. I like the ethical beliefs, but I have never really felt like I belonged.

It was 3:30 on a Thursday, and I was meeting with a rabbi in preparation for my big day. We were practicing the part of the haftorah that I was to read in transliterated Hebrew, baruch atah adenoid eluhainu. This was the part of the blessing I would read during my ceremony. At 4:00 pm sharp, at the synagogue, uncles, aunts, cousins, spouses, and well-wishers were waiting for the show to start, and I was sweating like a stuck pig. (Did that violate kosher rules?)

When Mom and Dad arrived, my mother was shocked that this synagogue allowed only men at the front, while the women were to sit behind a small curtain. Whatever sensibilities she had about this arrangement, she grudgingly sat on her anger, but later in the ceremony, I caught her peeking under the curtain at me standing at the podium with the rabbi and the rolled-out

Torah, giving my take on what I had read. I would eventually be declared and confirmed a Jew.

My anxiety was beginning to get the better of me. After the ceremony, everyone left the synagogue and crowded into our small apartment. At this point, I was developing an intense case of viral pneumonia. My fever had reached 106 degrees, so for the party, I was relegated to a back bedroom.

Maybe this is what I was getting for being a bad Jew.

The young boy who had said the haftorah had now graduated into being a man! All the guests came up to me with envelopes with money in them and told me "Congratulations! Today, you are a man."

Then, as each of them handed me an envelope, they told me, "Make sure you take this to your mommy."

I sure didn't feel like much of a man.

The Hidden Language

My father had a close friend, a drummer, by the name of "Specs" Powell, the first black man to become a staff musician for CBS in 1943. They had played together in a number of groups and on several TV shows, like The Johnny Carson Show. They held each other in high regard. My dad invited Specs to come to our apartment in New York for dinner.

As per usual, my father, after parking his car, did not go around to the front of the building (the long way) but instead went through the basement. Everything seemed normal and enjoyable to my father, but he noticed that, after that dinner, Specs remained cold and aloof. My father's gesture of friendship and caring seemed to produce the opposite effect of what my father had wished for.

Fifty years later, my parents travelled to the island of St. John where they discovered Specs and his wife operated a restaurant and bar. They reconnected affectionately and as barriers melted, with a certain amount of alcohol, Specs revealed to my father that when he was taken through the basement of the building, Specs interpreted that as a move to intentionally hide from the white people in the building, the fact that he was inviting a black man into his home.

Specs was *deeply* offended, and because of the assumptions he made, he never brought it up to my father. He merely withdrew. Toward the end of their lives, they restored the affection and camaraderie they had before this misunderstanding.

Puberty and Hypothyroidism

The stress of "becoming a man" or of having my dad as a bass teacher weren't the only problems I was having at the time in the early fifties. From the ages of about eleven to thirteen, my hypothyroidism had caused me to put on a massive amount of weight. This was an extremely difficult time for me—I don't really even know how I made it through.

Under normal circumstances, when a boy reaches the age about of eleven, his body will start changing. As a young man, his testicles will drop. He'll develop new body hair. His hormones will increase, his voice will become deeper in tone, and so on. At least, that is what is supposed to happen.

At this point in my life—right in the prime of puberty—my testicles still hadn't dropped, my voice was still high, and I had suddenly started putting on a grotesque amount of weight.

Gene didn't have any of these problems when he went through puberty, and my father—who had been 155 pounds all his life—had no tolerance for my condition. He grew angry with me and started shaming me relentlessly. My mother was just agonizing about the whole situation. She'd always had a pattern of putting on a bunch of weight—usually at the times that my father was being an asshole—and then losing it all again.

This was all happening at the same time in my life that I was becoming interested in girls, and I'm pretty sure I dissociated from all of it. I was certain I was absolutely grotesque looking, and I simply couldn't bear it. I don't think that I even glanced at the mirror; it was just too hard to look at myself.

In this dissociated condition, I redirected my energy into my own small business, picking up and delivering laundry in the many buildings around my home. This gave me a sense of purpose and guaranteed I would not have to spend much time at home where my father could be emotionally brutal toward me in my current condition. It didn't hurt that I was praised for this entrepreneurial endeavor by my customers.

I had to shut it down in 1954, when my father landed a new job in Culver City, California, near Los Angeles. I would be moving my massive self across the country. We began preparing to drive to what would become our new home.

While our parents were packing up our apartment for the move, Gene and I were put into YMCA camp. My father spoke with the camp counselor and told him to do whatever it takes to make me lose weight. There was only one other kid at the camp—a Jewish kid—who was overweight. For the entire duration of the camp, I endured mental and emotional abuse from that counselor. When I tried to communicate the abuse to my parents, I was ignored, and my weight was still blamed on sheer laziness and overeating.

One light that shined in all of this darkness for me was one particular camp teacher I had: Calvin. Calvin was a young black man, in his early twenties. He was short, studious, sincere, and caring. Calvin taught arts, crafts, and music, and he led the boys' choir. He was the only one around who made me feel valuable during my time there.

I was thirteen years old, and I was still singing soprano. Instead of stigmatizing me for this, Calvin convinced me to sing lead soprano. He taught me a lot about music, but more importantly, he just sat with me and let me talk. He reminded me that I was okay.

After what felt like an eternity, camp was finally over, and Gene and I were ready for the new adventure. My parents came to get us, and we began the lengthy drive across the country, camping out most of the way. I can still vividly remember arriving at Yellowstone National Park and taking my brother for a hike up the mountain to a place called Tuolumne Meadows, where we drank water from the glaciers.

Later that week, my brother and I spotted a mother bear and her cub, and just for the fun of it we picked up cans and sticks and started chasing them. I don't think we had any idea of the danger we were in until the mother bear turned, rose up on her hind legs, and roared. Gene and I turned and ran, silently agreeing never to tell our parents what had just happened.

Upon reflection, I realize that this trip could have been a wonderful bonding experience for the four of us. Unfortunately, my father was just not capable of that type of bonding.

When we arrived in California, my mother came to the realization that my weight must be some sort of medical problem. She took me to see an endocrinologist named Dr. Tobias. He immediately recognized that I had hypothyroidism, which explained why I was still pre-pubescent and unable to take any of the weight off. He immediately put me on a thyroid regimen, and my body began to change drastically.

I still have occasional crushing memories arise of looking at a photograph of myself in that overweight state and feeling utterly repulsed by it. Aside from that, the whole period of time seems relatively blank to me, clouded by the shame and humiliation I experienced.

CALIFORNIA

Culver City and Hawthorne

Whether I wanted to or not, I was facing a new chapter in my life. Around 1954, California would be quite the change of scenery for me after spending my first thirteen years of life in New York City.

After the extensive road trip, we'd finally made it to our new home: a rental house in Culver City, just outside of Los Angeles, where my father had his new job as the sales manager for a high-end, hi-fidelity tape recorder company. I spent my last year of junior high there.

One memory I retain from those years is my first experience of prejudice while being chased on my bike by a group of boys calling me a kike. My bike was faster than they were.

In Culver City I met Sandy Seigel in school. His family also had socialist leanings and he became a lifelong friend. He later was involved in the civil rights movement in Mississippi around the time I was.

From Culver City, we moved into a house in Hawthorne. It was while I was living in Hawthorne that I met an unforgettable man by the name of Mr. Goodfellow. He was a teacher at my school, and he changed my life completely when he put me in one of the first gifted classes in the country. He selected me because of my IQ and not my grades, which was a good thing.

For as long as I could remember, I'd always seen myself as an oddball who didn't seem to fit in anywhere. When I attended the seminar class for the gifted program, I realized for the first time ever that there were others like me in the world. Mr. Goodfellow devoted a good deal of the time in class to expanding our awareness of the world around us, teaching us about things like propaganda and how it applied in our political system.

We also learned speed-reading and attended classes at the University of Southern California and Pepperdine College. I began to flower and expand. I felt like I really belonged somewhere.

EARLY LESSONS
FOR BILL GOODFELLOW

We were so precocious,
Insistent little goats
nosing our way through realities.
    And you, located close to the Tao,
    Seeing beyond the vanishing point
        patient, not for us,
        but because that was the way.
I have glimpsed the quiet spaces,
The resonance you communed with,
And know the need to let it go,
The not-struggling that permits the universe
To reveal its sweet secrets.

Two or three times a year he would have a party for us at his home. His wife, Elizabeth, was sweet, gentle, and very bright. These parties were the high points of every semester. At one party we all showed up and danced on his lawn.

When he died, I was sick and at home. My mother took the following poem I wrote for him and read it at his memorial service.

CHANGE OF VENUE
FOR BILL GOODFELLOW

It is the flute's bewitching tone
    the subtle fire within
        that does not dim with age
And you, you sly old goat,
    you sleight-of hand medicine man
        tickled us to believe ourselves
I believed in your ability to believe in me
    Elizabeth convinced me that you weren't crazy
        when I saw the way she looked at you
I'm old enough to know your gift
    I practice your arcane art
        your person gardening
I hear your passage to newer slopes
    and pause in life's headlong plunge
        the flute's bewitching tone rings clear

⁓⚬ɞ᷾ɞᷚᵥᷛ⚬⁓

There were three distinctly different types of people that I found myself spending time with during this phase of my life—the intellectual type, the musical type, and the type that sometimes liked to get into a bit of trouble. One of my classmates from the seminar was a math genius. He would say to me, while standing in the lunch line, "If you would just let me divide by zero, I could prove to you that the Empire State Building is the Sphinx!" It was the kind of obscure humor that tickled my fancy.

At the same time, I had also been playing trombone with the marching band there. It was a top-notch marching band that ended up marching in the Rose Parade, and a new teacher had just taken the reins. I was not performing very well as a trombonist, and at the end of my first semester, my teacher had given me a C. This infuriated me. In this completely hijacked state, I confronted him, saying, "Either give me an A or give me an F." He gave me an F.

I knew that this interaction was symbolic of my inner turmoil and the degree to which I was sabotaging myself. It was many years later that I began to untie this knot inside me in therapy. In one way or another, I was selling 500 percent of my stock; presenting myself as extremely bright and then underperforming. Promising to deliver more than I was capable of completing. Selling 500 percent of your stock leaves you in a position of tremendous psychological pressure, which you can never live up to. I had a bad case of overselling.

I also made friends with a group of kids that liked bowling and stealing hubcaps. As different from one another as the people were that I was drawn to at that time, I seemed to be able to fit seamlessly into all three groups.

I had also met a girl in Hawthorne. Her name was Bonnie, and she lived about four blocks from my house. We dated for quite some time, maybe for about a year. I was getting hornier and hornier, and one night, sitting out on the lawn of her house, I tried to ask her for more intimacy.

She said, "What do you want?" and I reached out and put my hand on her breast.

She jumped up and ran, screaming and crying, into her house. This was more or less the end of our relationship. After Bonnie, I met another girl from Hawthorne—this one had a "reputation." She had big breasts and was willing to let me touch them, which comprised the only two criteria I was searching for in a serious relationship.

They say that a fifteen-year-old boy could get a hard-on over a pothole in the road. That was me. Friends and teachers warned me about this girl, but I paid absolutely no attention. The relationship was short-lived, but it started me on the road of mild obsession with the fairer sex or maybe anyone with nice breasts.

Despite any distractions I was facing, I had been doing very well in school and was flourishing. Something had to give. When I was about sixteen, my father and mother decided that they wanted to buy a house out in the San Fernando Valley.

I really didn't want to leave my school, but commuting from that distance was not a possibility. I put my powers of persuasion to the test and tried relentlessly to convince my parents to let me stay. They reluctantly agreed to let me stay with the next-door neighbor to finish out the rest of the school year. Ultimately, that arrangement didn't work so well.

As I became less organized, my grades quickly began to drop. When my dad saw that my grades were going down, he abruptly pulled me out of my gifted class and stuck me in a school in the San Fernando Valley called Birmingham High School.

I wasn't at all happy with having to move and switch schools, but there were eventually some bright moments and great memories that happened there, when I was seventeen.

⤬

BRIGHT MOMENT: I met a girl named Marlene at Birmingham High. We did "it" in the backseat of her father's Buick in the driveway of her parents' home, and we were both sore for days. We did not care.

⤬

In my relationship with Marlene, I had my first experience of family dysfunction outside of my own family. I made my first ever foray into being a therapist by attempting to help her family to resolve their problems. This so irritated her father, that he called my father and told him to make me stop trying to interfere.

After Marlene, my next girlfriend was Rowena. Many years later, when I reconnected with Rowena, she asked me if I remembered Marlene, and I told her of course I did. She was the first woman I had a sexual experience with. To which Rowena replied, "Me too." She then told me that her brother had also had his first sexual experience with Marlene. I was very grateful for Marlene and her openness.

Ultimately, I ended up graduating from Birmingham High School without any issues and went on to attend junior college at Los Angeles Valley College.

I tried to stay connected throughout the years in any way I could with the great people I had met at Hawthorne. We tried to have group parties at least once a year, but it could never really fill the void that I felt when I moved away from them.

Regrettably, I never got to finish what I started in that gifted class, and I didn't realize until recently how profound the effect was on me of having all of that taken away. It was a loss I could never express but had to bury.

Brandeis Camp Institute—The Lone Ranger

The summer after I graduated from high school in 1958, my friend Bob from the gifted class arranged for me to get a scholarship to attend a Jewish summer camp called Brandeis Camp Institute. The camp was located in Simi Valley north of Los Angeles. The food was kosher, and the music was traditional Jewish and Israeli.

I joined the choir under the direction of Max Helfman, who was the music director at Hebrew Union College in New York. Max was universally beloved—a sweet, caring, and humane man—and singing in his choir was a blessing. I made some good friends and met some delightful girls while I was there.

After the first month and a half, I was approached to become a camp counselor for the younger kids. I accepted the job with pleasure and was assigned as a counselor over twelve teenage boys. I enjoyed working with the children and developed warm connections with them.

My assistant counselor, Andy, was from Peru, and was a strong, good-hearted young man. We got along well and were helpful to one another.

One of my duties as a counselor was to take the kids horseback riding. This was a task for which I was well-qualified, having ridden exactly one horse in my life. I had no idea what I was doing.

By the time I had gotten the kids on their horses and had boarded my own, I could hear screaming. One of the kids' horses had bolted at a gallop, and I was the only one there in charge. Instinctively, I slapped my horse on the rear end, just like in the movies, and started chasing the boy, yelling "Pull on the reins, pull on the reins!" This only made him scream louder.

I can still recall the clods of dirt hitting my teeth as I was yelling, "Pull the reins!" I somehow managed to pull up beside him and grab the reins to quiet the horse, and then gratefully received help from my fellow counselors. It is amazing what you can learn from westerns. I was an instant hero—for the moment.

Tractor Accident

The climate at Brandeis Camp Institute was dry and dusty, and some of the staff people would pull a water tank around by tractor, sprinkling the area to keep the dust down. Andy and I had time off while the kids were at activities, so for fun, we ran up to either side of the tractor and jumped onboard. When we decided to jump off, Andy forgot that the wheels of the tank were wider than the tractor and he miscalculated his dismount. He was crushed under one of the wheels.

I yelled for someone to get to a phone and call the ambulance while I tended to Andy. My blood was pumping incredibly fast as I tried to make him as comfortable as possible. The tire had completely passed over his stomach. Within twenty minutes, the ambulance arrived and took Andy to the hospital. I was alone, and I could not stop thinking the most horrible thoughts about whether he would survive or not.

Before long, one of the counselors came running up the hill calling my name. He told me that the director of the camp, wanted to see me immediately, so I ran as fast as I could to his office. When I arrived, Schlomo Bardin was standing in the doorway waiting for me. Below his glaring eyes, the first words out of his mouth were, "If that boy dies, it will be your fault." He might as well have been saying "We're gonna get sued for the death of this kid, it's gonna cost a mint, my job will be toast and it will all be your fault, you little putz."

It felt like a knife was cutting through my gut. Everything positive and enriching from my camp experience came crashing down around me, and I was overcome with shame.

Some of my friends tried comforting me, but I was completely dissociated. Everything had become just a blur to me, including the end-of-summer camp ceremonies that were taking place.

A new friend I had made at the camp, Lauren, reached out to me, and—in a gentle and loving way—talked me through the feelings that were overwhelming me. This helped me to muster up enough courage to go to the hospital and see Andy.

To my amazement and relief, he was smiling and joking with the nurses. He'd been a body builder for many years, and the core muscles around his stomach were strong—incredibly strong. They probably saved his life. The doctors were completely amazed that there weren't any serious injuries.

My relationship to Judaism was already tenuous, and the shaming and blaming face of the camp director would serve to cut the majority of the ties that were left. Ridding myself of the shame brought on by that day would become a critical part of my personal growth work—work that could be found in the "To Be Forgiven" file.

One of the saving graces of my connection to Judaism was an experience shortly after Andy's death.

⁓ꙮ⁓

BRIGHT MOMENT: My father and I went to a concert at a synagogue in West Hollywood. It featured a high-powered Baptist Choir, the kind that grabs you and pumps you full of God. The room was rockin'. Max Helfman spoke for fifteen minutes. As the music director of Hebrew Union College, he was immensely qualified to speak about the universality of music. He then spoke about the blues, its warmth and inclusiveness, passion and transcendence.

The next session would start with a Jewish cantor singing a beautiful Hebrew melody, leading to the melody played by world-renowned jazz cellist, Fred Katz. Then, based on Fred's arrangement, Paul Horn, flautist, took the lead along with bass, drums, and piano, introducing improvisation. With the band behind him, Fred signaled the cantor to take an improvised solo.

My father and I were prepared for the worst. We were some stilted square pegs in a round hole. We thought combining a black gospel choir, a jazz band, and a Jewish cantor was a recipe for disaster. The cantor closed his eyes as if transfixed, and to our astonishment, exquisite notes, rhythmic swing, and celestial music came to us from his soul. This ignited the soul in each person in the audience causing them to jump to their feet and cheer. My father and I were overwhelmed by the shock and illumination.

Fred wanted the cantor to sing another chorus, and as any jazz musician would do, he said,

"Go, man."

As a classically trained musician, the cantor heard "go," so he promptly walked off the stage.

Bright moments are vivid and indelible forever. This one was technicolor.

George Oliver

That 1958 fall after high school, I began attending Los Angeles Valley Junior College. I was officially majoring in journalism, but I had also become interested in philosophy, social psychology, and girls. Not in that order.

Of course, I had always been interested in music. Los Angeles Valley had the best jazz big band program in the country, and I was joy-filled to be a part of it. I was playing trombone and a little bit of bass at the time. Because of the anxiety brought on by my father's teaching me, every time the band had to stop because someone made a mistake, it was usually my mistake.

It didn't come as a big surprise to me when Mr. MacDonald—the director of the band, as well as a kind and wise man—came to me and said, "Mark, I will give you a 'B' in this class if you promise not to sign up for it next semester." I felt ashamed, sad, and relieved, all at the same time, and I ultimately decided to take him up on his offer.

The next semester arrived, and we were about three weeks into it when Bob MacDonald came and said to me, "Mark, I am short a trombone player. Would you like to sit in for no credit?" I jumped at the chance, and strangely, without the threat of grades weighing on me, my performance improved significantly.

There was a wonderful jazz trumpet player in the junior college big band named George who had told me that all I really needed was a good teacher. He'd insisted that I see his teacher, a fabulous trombonist who had just moved to town and was currently taking new students.

I was reluctant because I'd had such a spotty, and disappointing history with music teachers, especially with my father. I knew that I was playing badly. Until I met this terrific man, I never really knew what a great teacher was or what kind of a difference having a such a wonderful teacher could make.

The name of this extraordinary teacher was George Oliver. He was a short and intense master trombonist. He'd played with the Chicago Symphony under Toscanini, and he knew all of the secrets that a trombonist needed to know in order to succeed.

I was very lucky that he was taking new students at the time. George had the ability to put me at ease immediately. He spoke in a choppy, Chicago accent and used simple metaphors to help me grasp the bigger concepts that he was teaching.

The method he taught was called "No Pressure." It put all of the control of the musical notes into four muscles surrounding the mouth. The more I built the strength of these muscles, the stronger my tone became. Within a month, my range on the trombone had gone up an entire octave.

Regarding my missed notes, George would tell me to think of a baseball player who hits the ball 350 yards, but the ball goes foul. People are still going to say, "That was one hell of a hit."

He confided in me a tale about a time when—rehearsing with Toscanini—he had miscounted, and at the moment when the entire orchestra was quiet, he played a resounding tone at the wrong place. Toscanini subtly returned the orchestra to its focus and moved on. At the end of the rehearsal, Toscanini came up to George and said, "That, Mr. Oliver, was the finest tone I have ever heard on a trombone."

My confidence and ability to read music shot through the roof. I finally had a real master trombone teacher. He would always tell me that he was going to show me something for my amazement—and he always did. Within a short period of time, I'd expanded the power and control of my lungs and was playing with a high level of proficiency. I had switched to playing the bass trombone—an instrument which I loved.

Although I'd started out at the bottom of the band, after only five months of studying under George Oliver, Mr. MacDonald would stare in amazement at my accomplishments and my newfound ability to punch notes and to help drive the band. As a reward, I was given a Bach Stradivarius bass trombone to use while I was there.

The First Pain

It was sometime around 1960 in Monterey, California that I first became acquainted with "the pain." It all began with my big toe. It hurt. It was not a big hurt but a noticeable ache nonetheless. It started at one of the greatest times of my life—age twenty.

It happened when I was playing second trombone with the San Fernando Valley Junior College Big Band in The Monterey College Jazz Big Band Competition in Monterey, California. Playing with this band was like surfing on a chocolate volcano. We were, of all things, the Valley Junior College Big Band, and we were killin' it.

Five days a week, my friend Mike Anthony—an up-and-coming jazz guitarist—would pick me up at my house, and we would drive to school, practicing our jazz by improvising, using our voices as jazz instruments or "scatting." There was a tonal alchemy between Mike and me that lets me remember those times as being "perfect."

SCAT SINGING

There is no distance between me
    and my soul
The music drags me
    out of myself
Shattered, birthing myself outward
    Always surprised
In love with my excitement about
    my excitement
Crashing into impossible tonal perfections

At this point, our band was heading to Monterey to enter the contest. We were primed and ready to go with great arrangements, strong confidence, terrific soloists, and me on second trombone—a position I had earned.

The night before the contest, I had talked my best friends Jim and Gene—a pianist and a drummer—into trekking into Pfeiffer State Park above Monterey in Big Sur to camp out in my family's tent in sleeping bags. It was ridiculously cold, and we froze our asses off. I felt the first little pain in my toe that night. It seemed insignificant at the time, so I didn't dwell on it too much. Besides, there was an upcoming contest that had my attention.

BRIGHT MOMENT: The next day as my band performed against big bands all over the country, I had a transcendent experience. There is nothing on earth that can compare to a seventeen-piece big band that is totally "tuned up." We tore it up—and we took first place for the best college big band in the country. To this day I can still feel the elation of that experience.

The annoying pain in my little toe from the night before didn't register in my brain as something to pay attention to, so I didn't. Besides, I had big plans to move to San Francisco in one month. To me this was the center of the universe and I was not to be denied.

Unfortunately, it was actually very significant. The pain grew into something quite substantial—it was the beginning of my lifelong struggle with psoriatic arthritis. For the first six or seven months after the initial twinge, I experienced increasingly bothersome discomfort. I realized later in life as I looked back, that as the arthritic pain increased, the focus of my experience shifted from one of expansion, joy, and aliveness to hyperfocus on managing the pain.

Before I finished my associates degree, a friend of mine named Jim and I decided that we wanted to go to San Francisco, so away we went, despite the pain I was feeling.

I had only seventy-five dollars in my pocket as I was getting ready to leave. My father was a very difficult man, and he decided then and there to suddenly insist on charging me for the medicines that I had been using for my arthritis. Luckily, my mother saw what was happening and stepped in and stopped him. I would have had to leave with absolutely nothing had it not been for her.

Green Valley Hotel

Despite my father's efforts to prevent me from doing so, I left home and joined my friend Jim in San Francisco. When we arrived, we stayed in single rooms at the Green Valley Hotel in North Beach, which was right above the Green Valley restaurant and bar. The Green Valley Hotel was situated on the corner of Grant and Green in the North Beach section of San Francisco, which was a very hip part of town.

My single room had a bathroom down the hall, and there was a nice little old lady who would come around about twice a week to clean up the room. The hotel was populated almost entirely by old Italian men. I loved it and thought that it was a great place to live.

There were people in the community—women, mostly—who looked after these old Italian men. Once a week, they would cook a big, extravagant meal—a genuine homemade Italian meal—and because we were staying in the hotel, my friend Jim and I would get invited to dinner to share the incredible experience.

I wasn't really playing much music at that time, but I did do a lot of listening at local clubs. The place we most frequently hung out was called The Anxious Asp, and it was a gay bar—something that we didn't realize at the time. I spent my days looking for work, and it didn't take long to find it.

Within just a few weeks of my arrival in San Francisco, I'd landed a job with Hooker and Fay, a stock brokerage firm downtown. This was a job for which I was completely unsuited, but I did it anyway.

I worked as a margin clerk, monitoring clients' accounts to ensure that they had enough value to be an asset to the company—at least that's what I thought I was doing.

Looking back, it would be difficult to imagine any job for which I could have been less suited. I didn't even like money. For God's sake! I grew up with socialist parents who believed that rich people ate poor people!

My boss at Hooker and Faye, a man named Dallas, suggested that since his parents lived in Los Angeles we should drive there and back together. The drive there was uneventful, and after we had spent some time visiting with our respective parents, he came to pick me up at my parents' house.

My mother had prepared a grocery bag full of sandwiches and chips and other appetizers. As we were driving back out of town, Dallas suggested that we should get some beer, so we stopped at a liquor store where he picked up a six-pack of beer. After we had finished off the beer and a few sandwiches, he stopped and got another six-pack of beer. I had little or no experience with drinking previously, and by this time, I was becoming quite woozy. As we pulled into San Francisco, I noticed all of the lights had gone fuzzy.

I was drunk for the first time.

He dropped me off at the Green Valley Hotel. The next morning, I got dressed for work. When I got to work, I realized that I was still half-drunk, and by 10:30, I knew that I was going to throw up.

I asked Dallas, "Would you rather have me puke in the office or at home?"

He immediately released me, and I went back to my hotel room. About an hour later, my friend Jim came through the door and I bolted past him to the bathroom and finally threw up.

As insignificant as this event seems, it probably accounts for the fact that I almost never consumed alcohol after that event.

In the Weed

It was around this time, about 1961 in San Francisco, when I first started smoking weed. There were two separate events with this. The first one happened with a trumpet player I knew. He had been in the service, and we would hang out pretty regularly. We got high one day and were just driving down Ventura Boulevard out in The Valley. I remember laughing the entire time.

The second event was just as memorable. One day at a bar in San Francisco, I met a Chinese guy named Sam Gi. Sam was a jeweler. He made jewelry that was so exquisite that he would often sell it to Miles Davis and other really upscale jazz musicians. He was phenomenal.

He had a girlfriend named Irene who was Jewish and about a foot taller than him. They invited me up to their apartment one night for dinner. After we ate, we smoked a joint. Sam darkened the room and we sat down on the living room floor. He took out a small, brilliant Tensor light.

⚬◦〜♍〜◦⚬

BRIGHT MOMENT: Sam turned on the little light and carefully laid out a piece of black velvet. I was entranced at this point. Then, he took two pieces of silver wire and put them down next to one another. He picked up one and bent it at a ninety-degree angle and put it down. He picked up the other one and did the same thing, but he bent it in the opposite direction. Then he picked up the first one and made another bend in a certain direction. Then he picked up the second piece and made a mirrored bend. At the end, he was holding two exquisite earrings. They were just beautiful. Every time he adjusted one of those wires, I literally saw negative space. I saw everything that wasn't the wire moving. It was a phenomenal experience.

⚬◦〜♍〜◦⚬

I went to my friend Jim's house to tell him of this incredible experience and he gave me a great, big lecture about smoking weed: "Don't smoke dope. You're not twenty-one yet, and if you get caught, your parents are going to have to come up here," and on and on he went. So, I stopped smoking.

Later on, when I came to visit him with my trombone, he was supposed to pick me up at the bus depot, but when I arrived, there was no Jim. I took a cab to his house, knocked on the door, and found him—stoned beyond belief. He had completely forgotten that he was supposed to come and pick me up. So much for my hall monitor.

Systems Awareness

I read a book, "Understanding Media," by Marshall McLuhan around this time. He explained the nitty-gritty of various systems within our society and in particular the impact of media in shaping behavior. He was the one who said, "The medium IS the message," And this has proven to be more and more evident in the world of social media, news platforms, and artificial intelligence.

Growing up in a socialist family, I was taught, and believed that "The System" supported racism, lynching, and unfair treatment of persons who were poor. It suddenly became very clear to me the way in which media operated as a powerful influencer that shaped our society.

This awareness became a context in which I developed politically, spiritually, and professionally. My mission became to make people acutely aware of the invisible forces operating on and in all of their relationships. I was drawn to tools that would allow me to do this.

I was intrigued with the idea of "Happenings." A Happening was an art experience in which the viewers became sometimes unknowing participants. Happenings were designed to make the participants aware of the systems operating in the game of life. It provided them an opportunity to shift their perspectives through unexpected interactions. In the 1960's, Happenings were being set up and performed all over the world.

Here's one. My friend, Jim Lowe, was a very good pianist. We once had him practicing in a beautiful onion-shaped church. When the audience came in, they could hear the audio recording of him rehearsing. Jim then came in and picked up directly where the rehearsal recording was, and began playing the concert live, blurring the distinction between rehearsal and performance.

When interviewed after the show, many in the audience reported an uneasiness, at first, that the performance was not following the standard format. They reported a heightened awareness of the rules of performance that were being violated. This heightened awareness was our goal. The whole idea of a Happening was to get your head to see things differently; to shift your perspective.

Jim and I formed a company called Love Power in Los Angeles where we performed Happenings. A Happening was also known as "The Process." In one of these, if you wanted to participate, you would pay fifteen dollars and enter a door. There would be a fairly big heavyset guy who would take your ticket and give you a form to fill out with some instructions.

Then, you would go down this hallway and turn right, and there would be a slightly bigger guy who would take your form and give you another one to fill out. You would follow his directions and so on, and pretty soon, you would have gone through about eleven different doors.

The guys giving you the forms and instructions would get progressively bigger and bigger, so you just knew not to fuck with them.

Eventually, you would come to a door where the guy would give you a receipt, and you would walk out the last door into the alley that dumped you back on the street. You had been "processed" by The System. The purpose of the Happening was to increase awareness of how people become complicit with "the rules of the game" and how this determines behavior.

Jim had a friend named Dixie. She was short with short hair, highly energized, and very opinionated. Her boyfriend John looked like a hippie with a long brown beard and long hair. He was a jazz bass player, a friendly sort. They lived together in the Potrero Hill neighborhood in San Francisco. Dixie worked answering the phone for a stock brokerage down the street.

Jim and I, along with Dixie and John, were sitting together in their living room when I noticed that there were long periods of silence, almost as if there were something going on but nobody could speak of it. I couldn't bring myself to even ask a question about it.

Then John suddenly got up, picked up his bass fiddle, and walked out the door never to return again. Apparently, John was tripping on LSD and had been processing his entire life in the silence of Dixie's living room.

This was my first encounter with the effects of LSD.

LSD shifted people's purpose for using drugs like LSD, peyote, mescaline, and psychedelic mushrooms from entertainment to soul-searching. These could be used to shift consciousness and change one's perception of the inner world and outer world. Years later, when I experienced LSD firsthand, I grasped the power of that impact.

Russian Dinners

In between listening to music at local clubs and working at Hooker and Faye, I also enrolled in some classes at San Francisco State University in the early 1960s. One of the most memorable classes I took was a course in Russian. I have no idea why, but I was completely drawn to it, and I was intent on learning the language.

In the class was a pretty and bright girl named Rita, and when the teacher of the class invited the two of us to his house to have dinner with his family, I was very enthusiastic to do so. There was only one stipulation—we had to speak entirely in Russian at these dinners.

The teacher's son was about eight or nine years old, and whenever we incorrectly attempted to ask for bread, he felt that it was his role to correct us. Each time we attempted to articulate our request, he would reply, "Nyet! Nyet! Eto khleb," which was Russian for "No! No! It's bread!"

One evening while we were there for dinner, the teacher took us into his study. I stood there and scanned the room, fascinated. When I looked down, I saw a row of books—thirty-six volumes—all written by Vladimir Lenin. It turned out that our host was a communist.

More specifically, he was a dialectical materialist. The foundational philosophy of communism was dialectical materialism. It was also the philosophy for about a billion people around the world at the time—China, Russia, all of the Soviet Union, even Pavlov, all followed this way of thinking. A materialist does not believe in God, but he or she does believe that there is something that moves throughout the universe—a kind of a dialectic process.

The main idea of dialectical materialism is that everything contains within itself the seeds of its own destruction, and that a new and improved form will arise from the ashes of the resulting destruction.

This cycle is described as the "thesis, antithesis, and synthesis." Within any given thesis—this could be any idea or concept—lies its own antithesis. Out of the inner conflict that arises comes the synthesis. Over time, the synthesis that arises is a higher-level concept, one that is superior to the original, and yet it has within it the seeds of its own destruction.

It was an intriguing concept, and I thought with the widespread practice of this philosophy that surely everyone would have knowledge of the subject.

I remember vividly being at a party with a bunch of philosophy students at Berkeley around that time and asking them if they knew much about dialectical materialism. To my surprise, they said that they did not. I was struck by their obliviousness to a philosophical viewpoint that was held by a quarter of the world's population.

What had started out for me as a subtle subterfuge to get closer to Rita unexpectedly became an intense personal philosophical challenge.

Second Chance to Become a Communist

The Russian dinners weren't my only brush with Communism. My friend Joe Byrd was a musician, a writer, and an activist. I had been invited by Joe to teach a course at the New School for Social Research. It was the California version of the New School in New York, which was a very radical teaching environment. They were very activist-oriented—very much against the status quo—and were probably being monitored by the FBI.

Late one cold, winter night, I was preparing to leave the New School and head home when I stopped by Joe Byrd's room on my way out. The room was dark with the exception of a few dim bulbs. It was the perfect setup for some kind of film noir—a stark black-and-white spy movie.

Joe invited me in and began a conversation in which he told me that certain members of the party—meaning the communist party—had been watching me. Not only had they been watching me, but they were extending an invitation to me to join them. The whole thing hit my funny bone. I told Joe that I had seen one of their meetings, and although I was flattered, they had the sophistication of a PTA meeting. That brought our conversation to a sudden close.

Strangely, my father and mother were socialists, with my father leaning more toward communism in the late thirties in New York. When Senator Joe McCarthy went on his witch hunt on communism, my parents burned all of their political books to avoid getting arrested by McCarthy's "thought police."

Pacific Grove

Over the course of the months I spent living in San Francisco, I began to feel more and more pain in my foot. I eventually began wearing army boots just to give me more support. The pain continued growing until it reached a point that I decided it was time for me to leave San Francisco. So, I packed up and headed for a place called Pacific Grove, right outside of Monterey, where I moved into a shotgun shack. It seemed like a more calm and peaceful community that would be good for me.

Pacific Grove was a beautiful place. I got a job working at an ice cream store called Cecil's. The owner was a Catholic man—Cecil—who had nine kids. He was also the only white member of the NAACP in town. Cecil took incredible pride in everything he did. He was what you'd call a mensch—someone who takes full responsibility for their life. I rode my bicycle to and from work at Cecil's until my arthritis got so bad that I just couldn't ride anymore.

Within three months of my move, I had become crippled with pain. I couldn't do much of anything. I felt I needed to go back to my parent's home. A friend of mine, Mike Hart, came up from Los Angeles to help me move. He put everything I owned in boxes and shipped it all to my parents' house by Greyhound bus, and I joined Mike in his Porsche. The drive down Route One along the coast in his miniscule sports car was excruciating. We sped down winding roads at the edges of cliffs overlooking the Pacific Ocean, and all I could do was hold on and brace myself. I could feel the impact of each and every hard turn we took.

When I first arrived home, I never even told my parents that I was in pain. No one knew anything about it until two days later when my cousin Ginny—a nurse—came to visit me at the house. She realized what was happening and exclaimed, "My God! You're in terrible pain!"

I'd been waiting for an appointment with a rheumatologist, but when Ginny saw my condition, she called and insisted upon an emergency appointment. Upon reflection, I'm really not sure why I didn't tell my parents that I was in pain. Every joint in my body was inflamed to the point that it felt like I was on fire. The only joint that was miraculously not swollen was my left arm, which gave me great company.

At my parents' house I embarked on the beginning of what would be an agonizing near-death experience in a hospital bed at home.

Reign of Pain

My doctor recommended that I get physical therapy in order to keep my joints from freezing up. My father and mother hired a physical therapist from the VA Hospital down the street, and he came to work on me. He had a perfect sense of how far he could go and of how much was too much strain or pain.

My father decided that paying for the physical therapist wasn't something he wanted to do, so he decided that he would do my therapy himself. With every move that he made, he pushed me to the point of screaming. It was so horrific that my brother would hide under the covers in his bedroom to avoid the sound.

My father had become my "physical terrorist." After one day of this, I found the courage to tell my him that he could never touch me again, and thankfully, we got the physical therapist to come back.

"Some pain hurts. Other pain alters." It changes your life.

When the doctor came, he would tap on my chest and my entire body would spasm in pain. How do you deal with pain when there is nothing you can do about it, when the pain is excruciating, and you have no options? What happens to you then? You dissociate—which means your being leaves your body. That's what happens.

Another thing that happens is very much like grief—it's when you are trying to bargain with God: God, if you take this away, I promise I'll be a better person. Yet another thing that can happen is going to the "dark side," which is to become bitter and angry. Alternately, another thing that can happen is denial—an attempt to bury the pain.

There is a line from a song by Leonard Cohen, "Suzanne," that talks about how everyone must be broken. It reminds me of what happens when the pain becomes so intense that your will is gone. It's like you're broken. You can come back, but good or bad, you will never be the same.

❧ ✦ ❧

BRIGHT MOMENT: In my bed, I spent quite a bit of time listening to KBCA, the jazz station in LA. I was enlightened by the music of Miles Davis, John Coltrane, Thelonious Monk, and a host of other geniuses. This was all music that I had never really understood before, but once I began to understand it, I was hooked—and still am to this day.

At some point when the arthritis had gotten extremely bad, my father bought me a television set for my room. I refused it and had him take it back. This was a decision for which I am incredibly grateful today, because listening to jazz was so inspiring for me; television would have only dragged me further down. I got to know the ceiling of my room very well. It was composed of gray wood, and I could make out the grain. I spent countless hours hallucinating on the shapes and forms I saw in the wood.

Some people who have undergone a great deal of pain can relate to the experience, but others, who haven't really known pain, have no reference to compare it to. One such person was a woman named Marta. Marta had no comprehension of what pain was, particularly the kind of pain from which I had been suffering.

One afternoon, Marta had stopped by to pay me a visit. At the time, I was smoking cigarettes and was lying there talking to her while using an ashtray that was sitting upon my chest. When I put the cigarette out, I slowly and arduously moved the ashtray from my chest to the table next to my bed. I was fighting against pain the entire time. Marta became irritated with my slowness and complained, "Why don't you just put it there?"

It struck me at that moment that she had no point of reference for what I was going through. I realized at that moment how grateful I was for people who genuinely tried to relate to me.

There is one such friend in particular who was extremely significant in my life. While I was in the hospital bed, a new friend from the Valley Junior College Big Band days would come to see me almost daily. This was a reprieve from the intense loneliness of the pain I felt. His name was Chick Carter and he was a full-blooded Cherokee who had been adopted into a Caucasian family. He was tall, lean, and muscular, with beautiful bronze skin, and long jet-black hair.

Before I had gotten sick, I'd taught him the basics of harmony. In no time, he had jumped so far ahead of me that he not only mastered harmony but had also become an excellent tenor saxophone player. When he would visit me, he would bring his tenor saxophone, and I would sing bass lines while he improvised. He often told me that I was the best rhythm section he had ever played with.

He was always caring and always interested in being of help to me, and I to him. For many months, we would spend hours together, with Chick sitting at the foot of my bed while I talked about philosophy. He wouldn't say a single word. One day seemingly out of nowhere, he suddenly began a conversation with me about philosophy.

Astonished, I asked him what had changed.

He looked at me and said, "Every time you talked to me about philosophy, it was like throwing a rock into a pool of water. I could hear the splash. After several months, I could hear the rocks go 'click' when they landed."

The rocks had piled up under the surface to a point that they were now landing on top of other rocks instead of just splashing into the water. At this point, Chick could speak philosophy.

I fondly recall another vivid memory of Chick, this one involving a neighbor. I had made friends with a young woman, Laurel, across the street. She and I had been having some great talks, and I welcomed the bond with her while I was going through that period in life in which I was suffering from so much pain.

My friends Chick and Fredda offered to hook me up with Laurel. A time was set for her to come to my house, mid-day, and for us to have an opportunity to consummate our connection. Everything was organized perfectly with one exception—Laurel never showed up. Nevertheless, I felt validated and supported by the fact that they felt that I deserved to have this sexual experience and made the efforts to make it happen for me.

Chick later went on to tour with the Beach Boys, and regrettably, he eventually committed suicide. I will always treasure my memories of our time together and be grateful for having had him in my life.

Both of my parents had continued working throughout this ordeal, so other than when somebody came to visit me, I was alone every day for about six months. When the pain was exceptionally strong, my mother would come into the bedroom and raise me to a sitting position so that I could eat breakfast. It would take twenty minutes just for me to roll over so we could raise the bed. This made my recovery all the more amazing when the doctors finally decided to give me a drug called ACTH, which was a steroid. The day after I took it for the first time, I sat up suddenly and thus began my recovery.

Ed Puplampu

At about age twenty-four or twenty-five, when my pain had become increasingly unbearable, the doctors finally decided to give me steroids, and I began to recover almost immediately. I returned to junior college in a wheelchair and rejoined the jazz Big

Band, but my right arm was frozen in place, stuck in a locked position near my chest.

I decided that I needed to set a goal for myself. In three months, Ferde Grofé was to conduct his Grand Canyon Suite at our school. I committed to returning to the trombone and being able to reach seventh position—which entailed using a fully extended right arm—by the time of the concert. I proudly accomplished my goal.

Once I was back in junior college, I met a man from Ghana named Adinortey "Ed" Puplampu. We met while attending a philosophy course taught by a Phi Beta Kappa graduate from the University of Southern California named Everett Jenks. Ed saw how I was struggling—not only with the wheelchair but also with the psoriasis—and he took me under his wing.

When I first met him, he was in his mid-thirties and he had a black belt in karate. He was an imposing man—a large man—with dark, black skin and an African accent. He had played congas with the famous African singer Miriam Makeba.

At the time, he was also managing a group of apartments in the San Fernando Valley called Lenox Village. He lived with his wife, Isolyn, and their two children in their house, which was situated at the front of Lenox Village.

Lenox Village was comprised of sixteen apartments and two houses out front, along with, of all things, a repurposed chicken coop which I would eventually move into with Cheryl, my first wife. The apartment buildings were yellow and were probably built sometime in the fifties.

I soon discovered that the light was really quite beautiful in the late afternoons when the sun was setting. There was a big field behind the apartments that often changed into a vivid persimmon color.

The house in front of us was rented by a motorcycle gang called "Satan's Slaves." They liked us—thank God—and were quite protective of us. The daily routine for most of them was to wake up, drop some acid, smoke a joint, drink three or four beers, and repeat "I'm SO fucked up," over and over again.

Right before my move to Lenox Village, I was finally able to leave the wheelchair behind. Ed had taken it upon himself to help see me through my tedious recovery process. As an integral part of my body-strengthening, he taught me karate to enough proficiency that I felt able to defend myself.

He also introduced me to African rhythms. He would give me a basic beat that I would play on the side of my bass fiddle, and then he would improvise exquisitely. Most of the time, it was so exhilarating that I would burst into laughter.

Later on, I learned that Ed was also heavily involved in political activities in Ghana. He had always had an air of mystery about him and he was a master storyteller. Luckily for me, he enjoyed sharing his stories with me.

He once told me about a time when he was driving through the south and had stopped at a gas station where they had separate bathrooms designated for "whites" and "coloreds." His reaction to the injustice he found there was to buy cleaning supplies and clean the "colored" bathroom until it was absolutely spotless. That was the kind of dignity Ed possessed.

Over time, Ed managed to convince me that I should move out of my parents' house and into one of the apartments in Lenox Village. My dear friend and mentor, Bob Bailey, along with a couple of Nigerian students, also decided to join me in moving in there.

Ruth was a mutual friend of Ed's and mine who lived nearby. She was average height and a little on the thicker side with very long chestnut hair. Ruth played electric guitar poorly, but she did love music.

As part of my own mind expansion, I had become interested in Indian music—in particular, the music of a sitar player named Ravi Shankar. As sunset was approaching on Lenox Village one evening, I spotted Ruth and ask her to come up and hear some music. Always inquisitive, she came up to listen.

I sat her on my couch in my sparsely furnished living room and with full excitement, told her, "You're going to love this."

As the music started, it got a little faster, Ruth jumped up and ran out of the room yelling, "It sounds like mosquitos!" Her interest and curiosity were not enough to keep her there.

Ed, Ruth, and I were all enamored with a wonderful philosophy professor at Valley Junior College named Dr. Jenks. The three of us approached him about studying privately with him. We asked Dr. Jenks if we could come to his house once a week to study with him. He agreed to teach us for the nominal fee of $25 a month, and every Wednesday night after his children were put to bed, he'd provide coffee, and we'd provide donuts.

As he introduced us to modern concepts in philosophy, we studied The Rise of Scientific Philosophy by Hans

Reichenbach. He clarified the weakness in the concept of dialectic materialism and freed me to explore more complex and powerful philosophical ideas.

In the intimate time together, the flow of information was intense. We were grateful that Dr. Jenks was so generous with his time and insights. He was also excited to have three students be so interested in his subject matter.

I became quite attached to him throughout the year, but when I left for San Francisco to pursue my many interests, I didn't realize I would never see him again.

The Unitarians
and My Early Research Career

Ed Puplampu invited me to a Unitarian Church around the corner in the San Fernando Valley. The Unitarians later merged with the Universalists, becoming the Unitarian Universalist Church. I had never heard of them, but I always did well when I took Ed's advice.

The minister's name was Paul Sawyer. He was a poet, a writer, and a wonderful speaker. That day, for the first time, I heard him give a sermon. He began the sermon called "The Upper Misscouli River and the Old Black Bra" by telling a story about camping with his family in their VW microbus.

Somewhere on the edge of the river, the van had broken down. Paul considered himself, correctly, one of the least mechanical people alive, and he had only one tool in the car—a small screwdriver. He went to the back of the microbus, raised the door to reveal the engine and saw only one screw that would match the size of his screwdriver. He turned it twice, got back inside the car, and it started immediately. This, he claimed, was a miracle. I had never laughed so hard at a sermon in my life.

I decided that I would join this church and that the best way for me to learn the real purpose of the church was to become a teacher in their religious education department. At the end of the sermon, I introduced myself to the religious education director, an Englishwoman named Til Evans. She had a warm and sunny personality: bright, intelligent, and curious. We immediately took a liking to one another. She gave me a few books to read and told me I could start next week. She introduced me to Paul, and by the following week, I was teaching third grade.

At this time, I was just coming out of the wheelchair, needed to work and I had an idea for translating brain waves into color TV. I approached Dr. Barbara Brown, a leader in the use of brainwave biofeedback for stress reduction. She was the author of New Mind, New Body and The Alpha Syllabus. I told her my idea and she was excited about it. She hired me to organize and conduct a grant based on my idea about brainwave biofeedback and color. Truthfully, I knew nothing about it; it just made sense to me.

She was more famous than I knew and she set up a lunch between me and Dr. Timothy Leary to talk about brainwaves, biofeedback, and the possible uses of LSD. At the end of the lunch, he said "Beware of the No-Game Game." Just that. People at that time had read a book entitled Games People Play by Eric Berne and thought they were transcending those games. Dr. Leary was telling me that this was a game in itself.

I was already familiar with The Tibetan Book of the Dead and Taoism but his simple idea enlarged the scope of my own spiritual studies exponentially. True to form, his comment opened a new pathway in my search for higher consciousness. The words from Dr. Leary would become an overarching concept that broadened the scope of my mind-expanding adventures in practical spirituality.

Before I could conduct my research, I had to finish a research project Dr. Brown was already involved in, which was studying brainwave patterns in cats with different personalities and comparing them. It also included looking for feral cats and fearful cats. So, picture me with basically no training, watching cats walking around the basement of a VA hospital, wired-up, with their brainwaves being recorded. The scene was surreal and would never happen in today's world of animal rights. At least I hope not. But there I was, working in research and volunteering at the Unitarian church.

Meanwhile, back at work, I had the "bright" idea to work with a blind friend to see if taking acid could help him develop some kind of sight. To do this we decided he would take acid, I would take him to the basement lab and we would use the brainwave biofeedback equipment to map his ability to visualize. In the middle of preparing the scene, Dr. Brown showed up, saw our unauthorized "research" and walked out. The next day, she rightly fired me on the spot. Had I been less horrified at getting caught, I might have actually been able to call upon her mercy, explain to her what we were doing, and not lose my job.

I needed work, so I went across the street to the Unitarian church and let them know that. I had been working with the children's classes, and because of a recommendation from the soon-to-be-leaving Til Evans, I was hired right then to replace her as religious education director.

I was genuinely interested in the kids and was excited to be working with them and the teachers. I was a playful person, and I quickly started inventing new curriculum ideas based on the work of Abraham Maslow, the psychologist and philosopher and author of Toward a Psychology of Being. Maslow coined the term "peak experiences": high points in life when a person felt in harmony with themselves and their surroundings. He believed that children did not learn in a linear manner but through peak experiences that allowed them to open up to new possibilities. In this state, lessons learned went deep.

My first invention was called a "Me Chart." I bought a bunch of crayons and had the kids put a picture of themselves in the center of a large piece of paper. I then had them draw lines from that center to representations of people and things that were meaningful to them. I showed them how to draw lines between themselves and Mom, Dad, slot cars, pizzas, God, their sisters and brothers, their friends. I then showed them how to select the colors of crayons that most represented the emotions they felt towards these various objects surrounding the centerpiece. Then we would talk about all of it.

Sometimes they might have three or four colors going to the same spot, which gave me the option to talk to them about having different feelings toward the same person. The thickness of the lines could represent intensity of the relationship. The distance between the center and a given object could denote degree of attraction or repulsion. Til was so thrilled with this idea that she submitted it to the national Unitarian Education Program, and they adopted it. Years later, at a lecture given in Atlanta by the director of the Unitarian Universalists Education Program, they opened the session by passing out "Me Charts" to the audience.

One day I decided to create something that would allow the children to give back to the parents. I called it the "Circus of the Senses." Individual adults and couples were invited into a gazebo where they were blindfolded and led by a child reading poetry, to another room which was pitch black. Once inside that room they took their blindfolds off and then colored lights and freeform organ music would engulf them.

Next, they would be blindfolded again and given a white cane to have a greater experience of being blind. They were assisted to another room where they were given headphones and a microphone set up to feed back to them their own voice on a five-second delay loop. This was very disorienting when they tried to speak.

They were then taken to another microphone attached to a machine which was donated by the John Tracy Clinic for children with hearing loss. The adult could speak into the microphone and hear themselves played back as if they had twenty percent hearing loss, forty percent hearing loss, sixty percent hearing loss, et cetera.

The final step of the "Circus of the Senses" was the invention of a lifetime—I called it "The World's Largest Balloon Sculpture."

⌛

BRIGHT MOMENT: "The World's Largest Balloon Sculpture" All participants were invited into the recently built church which was in the shape of an inverted onion. Imagine those long skinny balloons you can twist into animals. Now imagine a freeform sculpture made up of thousands of those skinny balloons twisted together.

There were some basic rules for building the balloon sculpture, among which were: you could not do it wrong; adults and children were equals in making choices about the sculpture; and if your balloon got popped, you got an automatic hug—this one was optional.

At the end of the process, the balloon sculpture was pulled down and stomped, first by little children, and then by bigger ones. I took great joy in putting on this "Circus of the Senses" and although I didn't know it at the time, later in life, the "World's Largest Balloon Sculpture" would make at least fifty more appearances from Atlanta, Georgia to Memphis, Tennessee and even at the Lincoln Memorial in Washington D.C.

⌘

Lawrence

While working as Religious Education Director for the Unitarian Church in San Fernando Valley, I decided to try changing my name to Lawrence. I'd been introduced to a man named Sam-Tio Chung, who was a master psychodramatist. He was a small Chinese guy, and he had a problem of some sort with one of his legs, which made him limp.

Psychodrama, created by Dr. J. L. Moreno, encouraged the participants to explore their emotions through acting. Psychodrama is a technique that allows people to bring to the surface a visible way of describing their inner life for therapeutic enhancement. It was revolutionary in the therapeutic environment of the time, and actually still is.

One of the roles is the director, the person directing the psychodrama. The second is the protagonist, the person the drama is about. There would be a participant who would be the protagonist's "double" and speak for them the things they were not able to say aloud. The rest of the group would take roles in the scene and amplify the inner dialogue.

Sam-Tio was a great psycho-dramatist and my kind of guy. We were doing these psychodramas in great, imposing mansions in the Hollywood Hills. I was hanging out with him pretty consistently. I learned the kind of stuff that you can only learn from either doing it yourself or watching somebody else do it rather than reading about it in a book.

One day, as we were sitting around a pool, one of the guys said, "You know, 'Mark' stems from 'Mars,' the god of war."

He then went on to tell me that I had a tendency to be a little overly enthusiastic. He informed me that I was sometimes overpowering and overbearing. He then asserted, "I think we should change your name."

Apparently, being derived from the name of the god of war, the name "Mark" was just too heavy for me. We talked about it and somehow came up with the name "Lawrence." What the hell, I thought. I'll try it out. What have I got to lose?

The next week, as I was going to the Unitarian camp, I was scheduled to be one of the opening speakers. About half of the people in the place already knew me, while the other half didn't. I turned to the audience and said, "Many of you have heard my name as Mark, but I would like to ask a favor of you. I am considering changing my name to Lawrence, and it would be really helpful to me if you would all call me Lawrence this week. I want to try it on and see if it fits me."

Everyone agreed, and for the rest of that week I was called Lawrence. There were only two of us in the bunkhouse. My bunkmate, James Larson, was one of the most socially inept people I had ever met. You could put him in the middle of a small group of lovely people, each having had a couple of drinks and cooled out and relaxed—and he still would not have a clue what to do. He would just stand there. He knew that he didn't fit into anything. Still, every morning, he would jump out of bed and say, "Lawrence! It's time to get up! It's time to go! It's time to get a shower!" I always thanked him for that. I always liked that he was willing to do that for me.

At the end of the week's renaming experiment, I returned to using the name Mark and thought no more about it.

Interestingly, sometime later, I would go with my wife to visit Jim and Maggie—friends of ours who were having difficulties—and we invited them to come and live with us in Los Angeles. As we were driving down the west coast in Big Sur, California, we came upon the Esalen Institute. It was like the heavyweight champion center of the psychology field. We decided to stop there and have dinner.

As we were walking to the door, a man with a long beard and a lantern crossed our path. He looked at me and said, "Lawrence!" It was—of all people—James Larson. He had been so impacted by my name change that he'd changed his name to 'Lars.' He had also moved to the Esalen Institute because it was one place where he could be as weird as he wanted and nobody would even notice because everybody else was weird.

Esalen Institute was an incredible place! Lars had gotten a job cleaning the baths, the hot springs that come out of the mountains. Half of them were clothing optional. People loved to sit in the baths of the hot springs, just looking over the cliff, down into the ocean. Lars had learned how to do massage and eventually garnered quite a following.

The last time I was at Esalen, I asked if anybody knew Lars. "Oh, yeah! Sure!" He had definitely made a name for himself. He must have spent thirty years or more there, living in a small cabin on the edge of a cliff, where being socially inept didn't make any difference whatsoever.

Top O'Topanga and the Bach Stradivarius Bass Trombone

One evening on the road in Topanga Canyon, as the air was turning cold, my Vespa was puffing up the hill and past a nudist colony on my left. It was dark with woodsy surroundings. Strapped to the back of my motor scooter was a large orange instrument case containing the most wonderful bass trombone I had ever seen. Because of the energy and lung power I was developing in karate, my teacher, Bob MacDonald, offered to let me use the junior college's bass trombone. Brand new. Gleaming.

As I opened up the case inside the Top O'Topanga bar, I was overcome with joy.

I was there for the weekly Sunday night jam session. All the band members were highly impressed by my Bach Stradivarius bass trombone. The gold was luminous.

On the bell of the trombone, you could see the vivid reflection of all the other lights in the bar flashing—reds, blues, yellows. We played traditional swing music, and the bass trombone lifted the band up. I was feeling very powerful.

After a couple of tunes, I decided to take a short break. As I was standing at the bar, I noticed an attractive woman sitting a few seats down. I was struck by the intensity with which she was listening to the music. Her eyes rarely moved from the stage, and she responded to some of the vocabulary of the nuanced jazz the musicians used.

In that first nervous moment, I asked her name.

"Dorothy," she answered.

She told me that she liked my playing, and we engaged in a form of bar talk that allowed us to make a connection. She told me that she was the mother of a thirteen-year-old boy, and that they lived on Malibu Beach.

The tone of the conversation became warmer, and we decided that after the jam session was over, we would go to her house.

Full of twenty-year-old juices and excitement, I followed her to a small house on the beach, and after some more talk, we went to bed, the ocean lapping at the beach in front of her house. Our lovemaking was intense but gentle.

In the morning, Dorothy introduced me to her son, Benjamin. He seemed very at ease to have a stranger in the house. I stayed and spent time with them until the late afternoon, when I headed back to my school in the valley. We had a few more liaisons over the next couple of months, but ultimately, we drifted apart and went our separate ways.

Years later, Dorothy would appear at my house unannounced, the furrows on her brow an indication that she was distressed. She came there, she said, because she was having problems with her boyfriend. He was depressed and somewhat anxious, and he had gradually gotten to the point that he wouldn't even get out of bed.

I taught her some communication skills, in particular, the concept of active listening—a simple, straightforward way of hearing the inner emotional life of a person. I told her that active listening would give her boyfriend the opportunity to talk about what's been going on with him and would help to draw him out of his dark place. After receiving my advice, she left.

She returned to my house three months later, telling me that she'd had great success in helping her boyfriend overcome his deep depression. As she was speaking, I was allowing myself a few moments of pride in my work and happiness about her success. I asked her how the active listening helped, and she extolled its virtues, saying that it was the best thing that ever happened to them. Just as she was about to leave, she asked me, "Do you think it helped that I secretly put amphetamines in his breakfast cereal?"

Ah! Pride goeth before a fall.

Becoming Socially Activated

In 1964, I was attending Cal State University at Northridge in Los Angeles where I was working on my bachelor's degree. I had become very interested in social psychology, and my social psychology teacher, Dr. James Craig, was the one who would subsequently turn me on to the concept of marathon groups.

I was in Watts amidst the chaos of the riots, performing community psychodramas with cops, welfare workers, welfare recipients, social workers, and college students—all at once. I was in my twenties by that time, but I had a moment much like the moment I'd had back in public school in New York when I became completely enraged at the sight of the white kids picking on the black kids. When I saw on the news that dogs and water hoses were being used on the black people in Birmingham, Alabama, something ignited inside of me once again.

I had formed and become the president of the Student Nonviolent Coordinating Committee (SNCC) chapter on my campus in Los Angeles. I had begun giving speeches from the back of a flatbed truck, and I introduced my ten-point manifesto with stentorian gusto. The local TV station in LA showed up, and just like that, I was on the six o'clock news, where some "expert" spent about five minutes trying to refute the ten points which I had written at about three o'clock in the morning the night before.

An interesting—and more than occasionally weird—group of people formed within our SNCC organization. Our arguments were political, philosophical, and practical. We were riding the crest of the revolutionary energy behind the Civil Rights Movement.

That summer, in 1964, was Freedom Summer. This was a profound experiment in social awareness that was generated by Bob Moses, the director of SNCC. Bob Moses, Stokey Carmichael, John Lewis and others knew that there was a national media blackout about racially motivated crimes in the Deep South.

They were determined to bring national media awareness of this activity in the southern states to the nation's attention.

Bob Moses's idea was to recruit thousands of white college students and thoroughly train them in non-violent tactics, begin the operation of "Freedom Schools," focus on methods of voter registration and safety factors, and then bring them all to Mississippi that summer in 1964.

During that summer, I would march on picket lines against Sears, Roebuck and Co. for racially motivated, unfair hiring practices. I was committed to a non-violent course of action, while others wanted more radical attacks on the system. The end of the Freedom Summer movement was approaching and I was totally committed to doing what I could, including eventually going to Mississippi.

Looking back on SNCC, I see a young group of dedicated people—agitated, committed, and occasionally stoned.

Crazy, Weird, and Serene Teachers: Bob Bailey

Let me tell you a little bit about a man that was a major part of my life at that time—Bob. His full name was Robert L. Bailey. In his work clothes, Bob looked like a janitor. No, he looked like a janitor's assistant. He was lean and small in stature with dark, luminescent skin. His piercing eyes gave away the immense intelligence within.

We had first met at the Lenox Village apartment complex in the San Fernando Valley around 1964 when we were introduced by Ed Puplampu. Bob had an impressive list of endeavors. He had worked personally with James Farmer, Founder of the Congress of Racial Equality (CORE). He had studied astrophysics with Albert Einstein at Princeton. When missiles were being tested, Bob was piloting supersonic jets to keep track of them. He had come to Los Angeles to take a position with Litton Industries, a massive aerospace company.

Bob and I became fast friends. He mentored me about women, life in general, and what he called "Negro-ology." Once I had become activated by the Civil Rights Movement and had started preparing to head to Mississippi for Freedom Summer, Bob decided to teach me the subtle points of awareness that were needed when entering into African American culture. He actually taught me a great deal about black culture. I already had a feeling for it, but he really helped to refine it.

He taught me that there are simple little things that you wouldn't even think about—like when you go into an African American person's home and you sit down on the couch—that can send a strong message. He told me that when you are in an African American home, you don't sit down on the edge of the couch, but instead you sit back, into the couch. If you sit on the edge of the couch, it conveys to the owner of the home that you think things are dirty—that you don't want to get too close to anything.

If, instead, you sit back comfortably on the couch, then you give the message that you're comfortable in the environment. Most white people didn't have a clue that the way they sat on a piece of furniture could convey such a message, so oftentimes they would walk in and sit on the edge of the couch. They would be insulting the people in the house and not even realize that they were doing it.

Bob and I started giving speeches around the LA area in an attempt to raise awareness and money for the SNCC and to educate people about the critical issues behind racism. We had an unspoken agreement: Bob would beat up the black people and I would beat up the white people. Verbally, of course. We were a dynamic duo. We spent long hours in the night talking philosophy, racial politics, and—of course—women. He was my guardian. He lived downstairs in Lenox Village, and I lived upstairs.

If I was upstairs with one girlfriend and another girlfriend showed up, Bob would skillfully divert her into his apartment. We had devised a signaling system of a using a yellow light in front of my front door that would alert him to my activities. He would quickly step out and engage them in long philosophical conversations until my bed was empty.

Mobilizing for Mississippi

My purpose in going to join the efforts in Clarksdale was to shed light on the oppression that was facing so many African Americans. A major push was to bring white students down to Mississippi to help register black voters in hopes that it would consequently attract the media.

Times were turbulent in the South. Up until Freedom Summer, Mississippi had been completely blacked out by the media with very little information being released, even though there had been several lynchings and many other horrendous things going on.

The Freedom Summer experiment was both successful and tragic. When the parents of white college students demanded information about what was actually happening in Mississippi, the media jumped into the fray, compelled to inform the nation about the tragic condition of black people in the South. This is what Bob Moses and his group had envisioned.

I had managed to raise $2,000 and gather 2,000 pounds of food and clothing for the cause. I prepared to get on a Greyhound bus headed to Clarksdale, Mississippi with all that I had collected.

Just as I was getting ready to leave, my social psychology teacher, Dr. Jim Craig, stopped me and urgently asked me to come to his office where he played an audiotape for me. On the tape were five psychologists who had developed a small group method called "accelerated interaction" or "The Marathon Group." They were using this technique at Camarillo State Hospital with institutionalized juvenile delinquents. This was a segment of the therapy population deemed most difficult, most rebellious and angry. The histories of these adolescents were sealed so that the therapists did not have any data on them. The governor agreed that these records would be permanently sealed. This freed these teens to move forward with the plans for redirecting their lives in a productive way created in the Marathon Group. I sat, transfixed by the clarity with which they expressed their new ideas.

I listened with great interest to the conversation between the psychologists who were giving this new marathon concept a go. It was an event that brought twelve people together for an entire weekend, and the only subject matter was to talk honestly and openly as adults. No agenda. No program. I was utterly amazed at how deep people could go while in that kind of container. It was fascinating how quickly they could drop their masks and stop playing games. I decided right then and there that this was exactly what I wanted to be doing when I went to Mississippi.

Both my mother and father had been very involved in civil rights long ago, but when I decided that I was going to go to Mississippi, my father was furious. He tried to talk me out of it and got angry, saying to me, "You don't have a plan and you don't know what you're doing."

In my eyes, his reaction was completely ridiculous. I was going, and I didn't care what he had to say about it. Ironically, my father was the one who drove me down to the Greyhound bus depot with all the donations I had gathered.

Just as I was about to get on the bus, he started to cry. He knew that there was nothing he could do to stop me. In that sense, it was a breakthrough for him. He had taken plenty of risks earlier in his life when he was involved in events relating to civil rights, and I think it was hard for him to realize it was time to pass on the mantle of social consciousness to his son. I was going to do what I wanted to do, and that was all there was to it.

The only time my father ever wrote me a letter was when I was in Mississippi.

ANOTHER MUSIC

I learned the other day
To see with open eyes
The face you used to
    Protect the face
    You're afraid to show
That hides the innocence within
You're dancing to the

Sound of frozen fear

Let go

Let go

There is another music here

༄ ꕥ ༄

Two Weeks in Mississippi

On June 21, 1964, three young civil rights workers—
James Chaney, Andrew Goodman, and Michael Schwerner—
were murdered by the Ku Klux Klan in Neshoba County,
Mississippi. They had been there to help register black voters
during Freedom Summer.

These three young men had gone to investigate the
burning of a black church and were arrested by the sheriff—a
KKK member—on falsified traffic charges. After being held for
several hours, they were released after dark. Once released, they
were chased and murdered by a group of KKK members. They
were buried in an earthen dam. Their bodies were not discovered
until nearly a month and a half later on the fourth of August.

I arrived in Clarksdale on the same day that their bodies
were discovered. I was struck by the fact that I was not afraid.

When I had first developed severe health issues a few
years earlier and had my second near-death experience, I told
myself that I was going to run toward my fears instead of away
from them. Because of that decision, when I went to Mississippi,
I was fearless. I felt utterly calm. The inner stillness I felt seemed
to come from the belief that what I was doing was the right thing
and that the risks were worth it. This was a state of mind I

experienced many times throughout my life when what I was trying to do was in alignment with my moral and spiritual values.

I showed up with 2,000 pounds of food and clothing and $2,000 in cash I had collected in California and began my two-week stay there. I was helping out in the Freedom Schools.

In a civil-rights community meeting led by Bob Moses, Stokley Carmichael, and others, a young, white, civil-rights worker stood up and in a poignant and sincere tone spoke of wanting to be helpful and maybe he could give some of his clothes to the people he was working with. This innocent generosity contrasted sharply with the life-threatening intensity that bathed every move we made in the hot Mississippi air.

A profound silence emerged. We were struck with the purity of the offer. Even now I can feel the oppression of a deep sadness showing itself in every moment of that silence . . . in that touching moment of self-revelation. Not a Bright Moment, but a profound one.

PUSHING PLUSH PLUM PLUMES OR
MAKING MOUTH MUSIC

Brown burnished red men
    smoking joints and watching
        every newly opened door
            waiting for Geronimo
                to tell the white man
                    to cram it.

In the Freedom Schools we taught people in the black community about nonviolence and provided tools to help them with their practical education. We also stressed the importance of their voice in the voting process and helped them register.

We were attempting to be helpful. In ways, we were only marginally helpful. We witnessed the pain that was their daily experience. Perhaps my own personal physical pain allowed me to experience some inkling of the awful, unbearable weight that was carried by our new friends, day in and day out.

～✦～

BRIGHT MOMENT: At one point, my friend Bob Jones told me a story. He said his friend from England came to visit him. As they were coming out of the airport, his friend abruptly said, "Take me to the ghetto." This was not hard, as it was close by. As they drove through the streets, his friend kept saying "What a phenomenal people. What a phenomenal people." Bob said he had never heard black people referred to in that way. When Bob asked him why he said that his friend replied, "Given the pain they have dealt with their whole lives, the fact that they can produce such astounding music, art, and their sense of humanity makes them phenomenal."

～✦～

Back in Los Angeles

After my first two weeks in the South, I was interested in employing the marathon group process in working the youth group I had begun to form in Mississippi.

I returned temporarily to Los Angeles and talked to several of the psychologists I had heard on the tape and asked them to teach me. One of them, a man named Fred Stoller, said to me, "I don't have the balls to go to Mississippi, but I will conduct a marathon group for you for free." I gathered up a group of civil rights workers from around the LA area and we held a weekend marathon group at my parents' house.

It was my first marathon group. I had convinced those I had gathered together of the value of a process I had not even experienced yet for myself. We formed one of the first mixed-race marathon groups in the country. We ranged in age from nineteen to fifty-five, and each one of us was connected to an organization or group pursuing civil-rights goals.

We met at seven o'clock on Friday night with enough groceries for the weekend and a certain amount of trepidation. Fred Stoller led the group in a way that redefined leadership for me. He laid down a few rules.

The Rules:

First, our goal was to speak to one another openly and honestly as adults. This turned out to be more difficult than we had initially supposed.

Second, during the breaks for meals and sleep, we were not to make "sub-contracts." These were secret compacts that one member could make with another with the promise of not sharing it with others. Secrecy, I was to learn, was the glue that held dysfunction together.

Third, we agreed that we had the right to describe our experience to other people, but only our own experience. We were to hold other people's experiences in confidence.

We laid out the time for breaks and meals in general terms and made sure of bathroom locations and then we began.

I found there were three distinct phases to the marathon group process: Cocktail Talk, Fuck the Leader, and Existential Aggression.

The marathon began with an intense silence. Rather than leading the group, educating, lecturing, or even setting up exercises, Fred remained calm and quiet. We entered into the first stage of the marathon group, which is approximately eight hours of what we came to call "Cocktail Talk." In this first period, we shared with one another information about ourselves that we had shared with others: social intercourse which was habitual, rehearsed, and surface-level. You know what I mean.

The goal of this kind of conversation was to keep things on the surface, to prevent the exposure of deeper or more intimate feelings or connections. For many people, they spend their lives operating in that kind of superficial social interaction. They do not even know there is something deeper.

One of the participants, a guy named Murray, who was experienced in group therapy, began to get angry at Fred for not taking more control of the group and directing it.

As the group continued to deviate from previous therapy group norms, Murray became more anxious and frustrated. Fred's response was to suggest that Murray take over the group. Fred made no effort to control the group or be in the typical authoritarian role of a therapist toward a patient.

This was a revolutionary shift that required the leader to let go of top-down leadership in group psychotherapy practice. People tend to attribute to the leader a kind of mastery and authority that interferes with the fostering of self-empowerment within the group. Fred relinquished authority and the illusion of control.

When the group reaches this stage and superficial masks start to crack, people complain about the leader as a way of deflecting from their own fears of being exposed. Fred made this move because the goal of the group was to foster self-empowerment and drop the illusion that the leader controls the power in the group. In a traditional group, Fred would have intervened and asserted control over the group and done individual psychotherapy with Murray. Instead, he offered Murray the leadership role.

After the initial shock of that offer, Murray began to lead the group through suggestions, exercises, and analysis. This worked for a while, but the group found him more and more irritating as we moved into the second eight-hour period. This is the phase that we called "Fuck the Leader." During this time, people's masks began to crack. Their typical defense systems started to fall apart.

One of the things that they engaged in was carom shots. A carom is any kind of shot in pool where the target ball ricochets off of another ball to move it or send it into a pocket. For example, I am being confronted in the group about not being genuine in my interactions. I perceive this as being judgmental and I deflect that by pointing out that someone else in the group is even more ingenuine than I am. The purpose is to pass on the judgement to someone else so that I am no longer held accountable for the effects of my behavior.

Everyone has gotten tired of holding up all the defenses against the fears of being exposed. In order to preserve their safety, the group tends to turn on the leader about not doing it right or being inept or incompetent or any number of other strategies to deflect from themselves.

Murray really became more and more exhausted as he tried to carry the weight of the group on his shoulders. The depth of emotional revelation began to intensify. We had all run out of defensive strategies. "Cocktail Talk" got more and more impossible to support.

I watched Fred's leadership style with great intensity as if watching a martial arts master who senses changes in movement and energy. That's how he was in the group.

I was in the pot with everybody else having the experience. I was no longer interested in the same old social bullshit and was also no longer able to hold up the defenses myself. I was seeing games being played out that I had never seen before. It was like a mirror showing me the habitual games I played to protect myself which weren't working any longer.

We were moving into experiential awareness and everything was different, even the language to describe what was going on. What I knew was that when I went back to Mississippi, I would be using this approach and I would be in the leader's shoes.

At one point during a break, I was standing with Fred in the kitchen, and I asked him if there was one quality that was most necessary and descriptive of leadership in a marathon, what would it be?

He said, "You have to be a mensch. You have to be willing to take responsibility for everything that's going on in the group, whether people are angry, hurt, sad, or scared. You have to be willing to break up logjams in which people are stuck and unable to break free emotionally."

We finished the Saturday night session with a sense of awe as we grasped the power of the marathon group.

By Sunday morning the group returned quieter, more self-reflective, and genuine. Interestingly, Murray, with no forewarning or reason, was the only one that did not show up on our final day.

The returning participants related to one another without surface defenses. When these defensive blocks are dropped, participants see the harmful part they have played in being dysfunctional in relationships. They were able to talk about deep relational issues and events and were able to forgive and release the hold these had on them and the others involved.

This phase is called "Existential Aggression," but the outcome is self-revelation.

Because of the alchemy of connectedness, the participants (and sometimes the leaders) reach a point when they have a peak experience that opens a portal to personal and spiritual growth.

For example, in personal terms, this directly affected my relationship with my mother. I was able to express to her how important and valuable hearing terms of endearment from her would be to me. Hearing "I love you." Giving me hugs. At first, she felt awkward and protested that expressing herself in that way wasn't the way she had learned to behave in her home. In a very forthright way I said, "I need these terms of endearment and have every right to them." From that day on until the day she died she never missed an opportunity to hug me and to tell me how much she loved me.

My peak experience was that a doorway was opened that allowed me to open my heart in ways I had never thought possible without fear.

Not only I, but other members of the group shared the same experience of what happens when we drop all our masks.

Marathon is being naked in life.

❦

WHO YOU ARE IS NOT WHAT WAS DONE TO YOU

Blunt force trauma to the gut
The heart
Shame-tipped spears

Mother bouncing In and out of loony bin
House of cards
Eyes daggers of rage
Then icy dead

Ascent, forever unreliable
Father living on the dark side of the moon

A repeating war that demands a turning to the wall
Away from calls for love and touch

Pools of little tears never shown
These shards of dark mirrors

Shining light you are
Golden majorette
Leader of a band of
Giggling gypsy children

Bringer of hope
Trumpets and Trombones
Drum beats that awaken the soul,

your true self

That is who you are.
Ta-dah!

⁓ ❧ ⁓

I felt vindicated in my intense belief in the value of being totally authentic in a safe environment. There is something utterly magical about a group of eight to twelve people coming together under these conditions. Profound changes are experienced.

The size of the group (eight to twelve people) allows intimacy to flow. If the group is smaller than that, in a way it becomes too intimate and scary. If the group is larger than twelve, often one or more of its members can feel anonymous.

Two weeks after the marathon—when everyone else from the marathon group left and went back to their respective schools—I left LA and headed back to Clarksdale, Mississippi, where I would live for the next six months.

Returning to Mississippi

One of the ways I would be financing myself during my stay was through the help of four professors who were teaching at California State University in Northridge. I had managed to convince them to let me do this trip as an experiential project, earning three hours of college credit apiece. This made up one semester of school and gave me enough scholarship money to go down to Mississippi. I also took out a student loan.

One paper I wrote for credit was for Fred Katz, a professor, musicologist, and internationally renowned jazz cellist, on the freedom songs of the Civil Rights Movement. I wrote another paper on the social welfare system in Clarksdale, Mississippi, in which welfare commodities were distributed by white plantation owners who refused to give out the supplies to black people who showed any support for the civil rights effort.

The third paper I wrote for credit was a social anthropology paper for Dr. Bess Lomax Haws. Her brother was Allen Lomax who collected folk and gospel songs in the South.

I also did a paper on educational programs for young children in Clarksdale. All these professors were impressed with the fact that I was willing to risk my life to go and do this.

I wrote the papers during the trip and made presentations on them to the professor's classes upon my return.

Upon my return to Clarksdale, all of my friends had left to go back home, and I was on my own in terms of white people, but fortunately, I wasn't alone in the community. The black community was very supportive of me at that point. I was never by myself down there because people understood the risks I was taking, and I always knew that I could rely on them.

I was staying in the home of a black woman named Mrs. Brooks and paid her around fifty dollars a month for rent. I didn't have a personal room; the bed I slept on was in the living room. Mrs. Brooks made a little extra money on the side by selling "white lightning," (namely, moonshine) out the back door.

We developed a very nice relationship during my time there, and I had delightedly taught her to read and write. I was also receiving a continuous stream of support from afar. Many of the kids and teachers from the Unitarian church where I had worked would send me letters and big sheets of paper full of pictures and writing, so it felt like having real, tangible support from back home.

Through the Freedom School, directed by SNCC, I helped people with their voter registration and worked with a youth group. My work with this youth group is one of the most beautiful experiences in my memory of my involvement with the civil rights movement.

During my stay in Clarksdale, I was able to conduct two marathon groups that were among the few ever done in the country to include all Black members (except for me). The results of both groups of mainly teenagers confirmed my belief in the incredible power of the marathon group.

Mrs. Johnson, the director of the early learning center in a local church, invited me to work with her. I had started a school for young kids and was teaching reading and writing and also children's music. I was playing the guitar at the time, and I loved sharing music with them.

There was an old abandoned house in the neighborhood that had some bunk beds and the teenage kids and I would all cram in there and sing songs. The kids introduced me to the music of Smokey Robinson and the Miracles and Major Lance. In return, I shared with them some of the freedom songs, along with some other music that I had been working on—folk music and such.

The relationship I had with these kids was amazing. In the midst of the fear and electrically charged atmosphere all around us and the horrifying issues with the police, we could still find joy and sing together. There was a sense of balance that grew in us from sharing our respective cultures. Many of those kids left Clarksdale and moved into Memphis and beyond, going to college and developing professionally.

There were other instances that were especially touching for me during this time as well.

⌘

BRIGHT MOMENT: I remember walking down the street in Clarksdale when an older African American man in his mid-seventies walked up to me and shook my hand. He had a warmth and dignity that impressed me. He looked me in the eyes and said, "Thank you." It was as if he was saying to me, "I get what you're doing and I appreciate the risks that you are taking."

⌘

It was such a touching and humbling moment, and I still tear up when I think about it.

Risky Business

One particularly sweltering day that summer, a man named Bob Williams stopped by to visit the house. This guy was about six foot two, blond hair, blue eyes, and he looked like a redneck to me. I'd never had this happen before or since that day, but I took one look at this guy and said out loud, "I don't like you." He looked back at me—a nice Jewish boy, a liberal from New York—and said, "I don't like you either." He had been trained to hate Jews and I had been trained to hate rednecks. Almost immediately, we became good friends.

Within three or four days of our initial meeting, we were in a car one night heading from Clarksdale down to Greenville, Mississippi to meet with Stokely Carmichael. I really wanted to talk to him about performing intensive group work sessions with people in the movement. On our way down there, we ran out of gas. (Talk about stupid.) There we were—two white guys who were obviously out of place—when a cop car pulled up behind us. There weren't any lights out there anywhere. We were in the Mississippi Delta in complete darkness.

Bob turned to me and said, "Don't open your mouth! If you open your mouth, they'll know you're not from here."

So I stayed completely silent. The cops were very nice. They took us to fill our gas can, then back to the car, and we went on our way, our heart rate and breathing gradually returning to normal. It was curious that from our rough beginning three or four days earlier, here we were now, risking our lives together.

I did end up meeting Stokely Carmichael, and he wasn't impressed with the idea I shared with him. A university psychologist had already been through Mississippi earlier that summer conducting psychological research on black people based on stereotyping.

This was the last thing the movement needed. It increased the likelihood of stereotyping Black people's behavior in a way that trivialized it, such as taking the angry actions in the Black community and pigeonholing them as merely unjustified "defense mechanisms."

The effect of this was Mr. Carmichael being suspicious and defensive about doing anything resembling psychology. The disrespectful researchers poisoned the atmosphere to the point that he could not see the difference between that sort of categorizing and what I was offering through intensive marathon group work. I was not seen, and I got no cooperation from him. Driving back to Clarksdale I was able to acknowledge Mr. Carmichael's great importance to the movement coupled with a deep sense of loss of opportunity.

Once the hot Southern weather finally cooled off and it was nearing Christmas, my friend Sandy Siegel brought two students down to see me from the University of California at Davis. They had traveled to visit me during their Christmas break so they could report back to their SNCC chapter.

One of these friends, a woman named Joan, was a student at the University of California with whom I'd formed a close relationship—nudge, nudge, wink, wink. They had been driving many hours. Sandy reported that his tongue felt like the Russian Army had walked across it. Bruce, the other companion, was quite frightened since he was sporting a beard and was in a vehicle with out-of-state tags. This represented an outside agitator to the locals, so he spent part of the journey through Mississippi lying on the floorboard in the back of the car.

While visiting, they helped out with the Freedom School, taught language skills, and documented the kind of experience they were having in this scary milieu. Bruce and Sandy stayed about a week and Joan remained in Mississippi.

I vividly remember getting arrested while Joan and I were just standing on the porch of Mrs. Brooks's house. The police alleged that I had violated the curfew, even though I wasn't even on the street; I was at the house! I was getting a taste of what kind of things went on in the "Black part of town." Joan and I were both arrested that evening—around nine o'clock—and we stayed in jail until around about two or three o'clock in the morning.

The man who lived next door to Mrs. Brooks was named Reverend Cooper. He was the one who came down to the jail to get Joan and me out that night. It was just the two of us in a single grimy cell. It was not pleasant, but I must say, even though I probably should have been, I was not afraid. It's very interesting how when you're doing something in which you completely believe, the possibility of death doesn't really make that much of a difference. If I were going to die, this would be the way I would want to go—doing something I believed in totally and completely. Joan and I became quite close, and she decided to stay in Clarksdale with me until I returned home in March.

The End of Freedom Summer

The day before Joan and I left by bus to return to California, she came back to Mrs. Brooks's house and brought in a small black puppy. The vulnerability of that little dog touched me at the soul level. The effect was startling and deep. I began to weep and couldn't stop myself for twenty minutes. It finally struck me that I was going home and that this phase of my life was coming to an end.

I became painfully aware of my closeness to Mrs. Brooks, Reverend and Mrs. Cooper, and a number of freedom workers I had spent so much time with. I also became acutely aware of the danger I had been in, which I had never fully integrated. Joan and I held each other and felt the aliveness of that moment.

Mrs. Brooks had become such a good friend to me during my time at her home. She looked after me with a loving heart and great generosity. After we left that March, I would come back to visit about four times a year for quite some time. On one of my visits, thirty years later, Mrs. Brooks looked me in the eye and for the first time asked me, "Do you know I love you?" I can say without a doubt that I knew. I felt an immense amount of gratitude.

❧ ⚶ ☙

Morgan Freeman has had a restaurant and a blues club in Clarksdale, and there are African American mayors there running things. These things were impossible to conceive of during the time of Freedom Summer. During Freedom Summer, if somebody had told me that we were going to have a black president by 2008, I would have laughed. Impossible! I would have thought. Maybe thirty years down the line, or fifty, but not so soon. The night President Obama was inaugurated was like a dream come true!

The Freedom Summer movement turned out to be very significant because it was so effective. It brought an enormous amount of media attention to the area which was desperately needed. While it didn't fix everything, it did make a difference. I learned so much in that environment, and the time I spent there was life-changing.

There is a quality of richness to the civil rights movement that's far deeper than a bunch of people just showing up and sitting in. There is something about people standing up for their own dignity that is absolutely priceless. The principles of nonviolence are deep and profound, and not many people understand them.

I've been a student of Gandhi, Martin Luther King Jr., and others who promote nonviolence and peaceful protest. This is actually spiritual development. It's not a technique to be used but an attitude towards life. It is standing up for one's rights and beliefs and doing it in a way that is not harmful. It's profound.

Since I was no longer afraid of death, I had no fear of what was going to happen. I knew that those three men that had died right before I got there knew the risks they were taking. They knew exactly what they were going up against. They were taking exceptional risks, and they were prepared to face the consequences. I have great admiration and respect for those three men.

I believe that if I had not gone through what I went through, I would be very "vanilla." I would be boring. I wouldn't be a risk taker. In my own case, I put myself out there the way I did because I believed in the cause.

Ultimately, what I experienced in Mississippi ended up helping me in many other aspects of life, such as when I was working toward my master's degree and my PhD. I ran into many difficulties, but after all that I had been through in Mississippi I was truly strong, and I knew how to organize. I wasn't afraid and didn't back down. The experience taught me an enormous amount about not taking shit from anybody.

In 1994 my friend Sandy and I went to Jackson, Mississippi for the thirtieth anniversary of Freedom Summer. Sandy and I saw ourselves as "elders" in the movement. We were completely delusional about the importance of what we had to say. From our very first encounters with the young students actively engaged in community service and development in Jackson, we got the message loud and clear. "We know what we're doing. We're good at it. We're dedicated and not that interested in what you old fogies have to say."

Sandy and I became very quiet and came away from that experience feeling enlightened. These students were in the trenches dealing with difficult political and social forces. Our drive back to Memphis was relatively quiet.

It wasn't until years later in discussions with Sandy that I realized I approached my time and experience in Mississippi as a spiritual seeker while Sandy approached it as a political activist. That made the effect of that experience totally unique. For me it was a time of profound spiritual growth.

Brother Lenny in Watts

After returning to California from Mississippi, I wanted to continue doing work in social activism. I had been working in an area of Los Angeles called Watts, populated mostly by African Americans and Mexican Americans. When things got really heated in the civil rights movement, there were a lot of places that were burned and several riots that took place. The chaos that ensued is known as the Watts riots.

While I was working in Watts, I had some really strong people around me who believed in me—and I believed in them. My good friend Bob Bailey had approached me about contributing my services to a new organization in Watts. A small group of African American men had organized a storefront training center called Operation Bootstrap. It was community-based and they received no federal or state funding. Operation Bootstrap was funded by a couple of corporations that participated in different ways. Bob wanted me to work as a Group Communications Specialist teaching people how to handle the deep emotional needs for connection among the participants. I started working with people in an effort to train them in new skills.

The leaders of Operation Bootstrap managed to convince the Singer Sewing Machine Company to provide us with a number of commercial sewing machines and training on how to operate them. With these, we could train people in the kind of work that would actually help them to secure jobs. In addition, Operation Bootstrap had managed to get funding for early computers and trainers from IBM.

It was a storefront in the middle of a very depressed area. Since we had no government money, once we started it, we got help whenever and wherever we could. One goal was to empower the participants to have competitive skills in the workforce as well as providing a new paradigm centered around self-empowerment. African American entrepreneurship was a focus and learning how the economic game was played was crucial.

During the next six months, I conducted community psychodramas with welfare workers, welfare recipients, social workers, and police. There would be as many as eighty people at a time in the workshops. I would lead them through exercises and psychodramas that allowed them to open up a conversation aimed at resolving problems rather than exacerbating them. We did psychodramas almost every night. It was electric. There were outbursts of emotion, tears, and reconciliation.

We weren't very far from the University of Southern California, which was a very upscale school. One of our goals was to enlighten the people of the white community about what life was really like for the people of the Black community. I was the go-between in this venture—I was the white boy between the leadership and the communities.

I had been working closely with a guy named Brother Lenny. He was always dressed in black, and he had a black pickup truck with a gun rack mounted to it, complete with a rifle! He travelled all around town with other men listening to the police band on the radio, following where arrests were taking place and ensuring that there was no police brutality. That's a daunting job to be doing.

Brother Lenny and I worked to bring white college students from the University of Southern California into the Operation Bootstrap program and introduce them to the conditions faced by the Black community on a daily basis. On one occasion, we brought in about twenty of these students into a fairly small room so that everybody was really packed together. Brother Lenny looked around at the faces and said, "You're here because you're interested in finding out what the Black experience is like, about what we deal with."

He then reached into his pocket and pulled out a paper cup that was folded over at the top. He quietly opened it up and suddenly poured a bunch of cockroaches out. As soon as those cockroaches hit the floor, the girls jumped to the ceiling! They were terrified. At their homes, they had people to get rid of these things!

It reminded me of the time I was living in Clarksdale. I had woken late at night and gone to get a glass of water. When I flipped on the light switch, the floor was covered with cockroaches. For someone like me, it was a total shock. I had never seen anything like that before in my entire life.

Much like that night was for me, this glimpse at an alternate reality was a violent shock to the system for these young college students. Unfortunately, it was a pretty accurate picture of what lots of these people living in the ghetto were actually dealing with.

My First Encounter with Mental Illness, Alcoholism, Race, and Truth

Every week, Operation Bootstrap would conduct a community awareness group designed to elicit feedback from the community and to reaffirm the goals and philosophy of the organization. At each meeting, a slight, intense Black man from the streets would stand up and speak in a rambling, disjointed manner about the activities of the organization. This man was clearly schizophrenic and also an alcoholic.

Once a year, a group of white and Black businessmen would come to Watts and pick him up to take him to corporate headquarters where they would dry him out and have him make corporate decisions. Evidently, when sober, his mind was amazing. Apparently, at some point in time, he had built a powerful organization. Unfortunately, the operation of it had created sufficient stress to activate his mental health disease process. Eventually, he would end up back in Watts, drinking and disjointed once again.

After I got over the initial shock of my abrupt shift in perspective of this man—from seeing him as a victim to seeing him as a success—I began to listen very carefully to his rambling monologues at the meetings and received a profound insight into the nature of schizophrenia. If you listened closely as he rambled, you could hear accurate and thoughtful observations about some of the key problems within the organization, but as part of his illness, he masked it in this "crazy" style of communication.

I began to see that—from a systems viewpoint—schizophrenia serves the purpose of allowing the person who is suffering from it to speak the truth in a crazy way, which—ultimately—protected him. I carry this lesson with me to this day. It helps me to remember to listen carefully to the logic within apparent chaos.

Charisma-Building: Lessons from Lew

I was in my senior year at Cal State when I took a class with master psychodramatist and coach Lew Yablonsky. He was an imposing pale man with steely blue eyes, bright and gutsy and truly devoted to the development of creative and effective psychological tools for healing every stratum of society. He had authored the book The Violent Gang, for which he had interviewed gang members extensively. He had a rough childhood and hung around many people he would later, after getting his formal education, characterize as sociopaths. He credits his rough childhood for his ability to see the complexity in people and for inspiring his belief in treatment over punishment.

Lew emphasized street level immersion and I participated in every psychodrama he conducted and volunteered for every role I could take. I completely agreed with his belief that great and useful social psychology should emerge from immersion in the social environment.

I learned a lot from Lew, not the least of which was how to stand up to him, an overbearing prick. This has served me well over the years.

One day he came into the classroom with the intention of giving us a device to help us establish leadership and charisma. He suggested that we locate the most insecure-looking man in the room. We should then walk up to him face-to-face and ask him, "How long have you hated your father?"

The odds were extremely high that this person would reply with, "How did you know that?"

Lew then said, "Turn around and walk away, saying 'Never mind that now.'" As I think back on it, this may have been one of the reasons I didn't like him. He used his leadership ability of being a director in psychodrama to intimidate and increase a fearful awe in the participants. He struck me as manipulative.

Nevertheless, I had many opportunities to practice being a psychodrama director and was able to participate in very constructive sessions. Although we never seemed to get along very well, at the end of the year, Lew said to me in front of the entire class, "Mark, I don't like you—and I'm giving you an A."

Joan, the Mountain

I had been deeply involved in Operation Bootstrap since returning from Mississippi in1967. I had maintained a close relationship with Joan, who had been with me and gave me the puppy in Clarksdale. I convinced her to join me in a weekend marathon group conducted by George Bach and Fred Stoller that was being held at a beautiful home in Palo Alto, California.

That Saturday afternoon when we were on a break and Joan had gone to use the bathroom, George, who was born in Germany, turned to me and said, "In Europe, we number the mountains from one to ten by the level of difficulty. If you are a 'three' mountain climber, and die trying to climb a 'nine' mountain, no one feels sorry for you, they just think you're stupid. You are a 'three' mountain-climber, and Joan is a 'nine' mountain."

His assessment panned out within the next five weeks. We had decided to meet on the coast between Davis, California where Joan lived, and Los Angeles where I lived. We had planned a romantic interlude and had just finished dinner and were returning to our motel when two policemen in a police car pulled up and offered us a ride. We gratefully, although somewhat warily, accepted their offer. I had previously spent very little time on the friendly side of police encounters. Nevertheless, it was a long walk and we could use the assistance.

Shortly thereafter, the police pulled up behind a camper that was driven and populated by Mexican Americans. As if a reflective bad dream were occurring that spoke to all of the roots and issues we dealt with in Mississippi, the police began beating up the Latino men.

Joan and I were both in shock, frozen and unable to act. Shortly thereafter, the police stopped their attack, got back in the car, and drove on in silence. I said nothing. Something shifted in my relationship with Joan that night when she turned to me and said, "My husband, Frank, would have done something."

The fear of being in a pitch-black area with two armed, violent policemen showed me how close I was to the primal terror I had thought was specific to the South.

I was disappointed in myself and felt shame at my inaction. That was our last romantic interlude.

Attack Therapy—Synanon Games

One of the most well-known and influential group therapists in the Los Angeles area was Dr. George Bach. He was a student of psychodrama and had developed an approach to group therapy he referred to as "Attack Therapy." Dr. Bach, along with Dr. Yablonsky, started Synanon, an innovative drug rehabilitation program owned and operated by recovering drug addicts. An essential premise of Synanon was that drug addicts were so thoroughly at the mercy of their addiction that they would put anything at risk — family, friends, children, and their own lives—in order to get their fix.

Membership at Synanon was established quite simply: You showed up requesting help, and they put you on a couch in the living room, provided you with minimal food, and required that you go cold turkey. This meant that, at any given moment, one could be walking through the living room on the way to the kitchen and there would be someone on the couch screaming and crying—begging for help—but members of Synanon knew that this was just the price you had to pay in order to demonstrate your commitment to the program.

A primary premise of the Synanon Games, a central tool in the rehab process, involved placing addicts in a high-intensity pressure cooker where veterans in the program verbally attacked new members with the express purpose of ripping away their ego defenses. The tone of the language was "I've been everywhere you've been, I've seen everything you've seen, I've used every trick in the book, and I'm not letting you get away with it." In other words, "Drop the bullshit."

Every day, the staff members would meet, go through their own Synanon Games and have the advantage of coaching from George or Lew. Then all addict members of the Synanon groups would meet for three hours of intense attack. Everyone's ego was fair game.

As part of my assignments in Social Psychology at Valley State College—now California State University, Northridge—I got to interview members of the "Synanon Games," as they had come to be called. The director, Charles Dederich, was notoriously powerful in these games and had the ability to take people from the violent environment of Hells Angels groups and break them down into sobbing children.

Everyone who participated in Synanon had a job, such as operating a gas station, feeding others, handling public relations for the organization, etcetera.

A number of well-known Synanon jazz musicians performed in the evenings to raise money and spread the word about Synanon and its effectiveness. Synanon would later lose credibility after declaring itself a religion and being linked to a series of violent episodes. Power corrupts and absolute power corrupts absolutely, they say.

Lew arranged for George Bach to start teaching at Cal State, Northridge. This was George's first academic position. As part of his psychodrama background, he came to school a day early to experience the college and meet people. He had the belief that it would help him in feeling more comfortable in the environment and more prepared for the educational requirements. He generally was someone who practiced what he preached.

George was notorious for doing therapy groups with couples in which he had everyone sitting on rolling chairs. When he felt people were avoiding the normal conflicts of a relationship, he would get behind one chair and push it into another like bumper cars, to generate conflict so that people could learn to handle it.

George also gave me another piece of self-motivational wisdom in private. He said that sometimes in the middle of the day, he would have a personal sexual interlude with someone outside of the group to give him something to think about when he was having a boring afternoon. What a funny guy.

Marrying Cheryl

I met Cheryl at Cal State University, Northridge before I left for Mississippi. She was a fellow student who also was socially active in the civil rights arena. I was president of SNCC and Cheryl had stepped in to take my place while I was away that summer. She had an infectious smile and was quite bright and pretty.

Within six months of my return to California, we had become very bonded and decided to get married.

I was a Jewish father's worst nightmare, specifically for Cheryl's dad. I was a recovering Jew teaching religious education at a Unitarian church. I was an ultra-liberal, and he never showed much cordiality towards me. He refused to come to our wedding, and he must have fainted to see that our first house in Van Nuys was a refurbished chicken coop. Some people would refer to it as a shotgun shack.

The living room had a meditation center. The kitchen was sparse with an old pot-marked stove. The bathroom always looks like it could use a cleaning. The bedroom was glowing, with psychedelic stripes across a slanting roof. The second bedroom was more conservative, with straight lines, muted tones, no-frills furniture. There was a back room which Ed and I used for working on karate moves. It was a big chicken coop.

LSD and Elliot Gehr

My first experience with acid was south of Monterey in Big Sur, California, sometime around 1965. It happened at Pfeiffer State Park, a beautiful campground right on the edge of the Pacific Ocean. Cheryl and I met a friend, Elliot Gehr, and his wife Elva there. Elliot had brought the LSD. All acid was LSD back in those days. After taking the drug, Cheryl and Elva, sometimes called "Moose," stayed low in the park and I spent some time walking on pathways up in the mountains with Elliot.

Elliot had already experienced LSD. As we walked up the mountains, the LSD kicked in and I remember vividly turning to him on that mountain pathway saying that I could see an infinity of pathways I could walk over the valley. He took my hand and said, "That's the acid, don't do anything." I assured him that I loved the experience and I valued life too much to do anything that stupid.

About two months later I was helping present two separate week-long workshops at a Unitarian camp up in the mountains around LA. I had gone up there with Cheryl. While I was there, Elliot was also a presenter.

The first week's workshop I had come to help present with my friend Elaine. This one, for adults, consisted of exercises with Zen, mind expansion, and spirituality, and it went well.

The second week was designed for adults, children and teens. I was doing some really great stuff: getting kids to make musical instruments out of things in the forest—drums, horns, all kinds of stuff—and then forming a parade and leading them down the side of the mountain. Elliot was an artist, and he was helping them express themselves through painting.

The teenagers didn't fit in with the younger kids or the adults at the camp, so they formed their own subgroup of people. They already belonged to what was called Liberal Religious Youth (LRY). It was something like a Sunday school group in the Unitarian church. They were very hip, very smart, very aware—and they also smoked dope.

Unbeknownst to me and Cheryl, and beyond any sort of good judgment, Elliot had promised these teenagers that he would bring them some acid. And he did. And he gave it to them. And they took it. Once I learned what was going on, I asked, "Elliot, what did you do?"

These teenagers were wandering around seriously tripping. I would walk around and see things like a rock with the word "rock" painted on it—now, that's acid talking. Some of these kids started to freak out. Cheryl and I—along with Elliot and Elva—had to gather and babysit twenty teenage kids who were all on acid. We were cooling them out, calming them down, patting them, and telling them that it was going to be okay. We all went on a trip, theirs different from ours.

Inevitably, one of them went to their parents and told them what was going on. By the time the adults got wind of the situation, the kids had come down from their high, but Elliot and his wife had to leave town after the fiasco. His father was a Unitarian minister and Elliot was an artist, truly with the best—if not well thought out—intentions. He packed up and moved to Eugene, Oregon to begin the next chapter of his life.

The FBI Chase

My friend Ed Puplampu's brother had been working for a rich family somewhere in LA as a house sitter. A child had been kidnapped at this home and he was a suspect in the kidnapping. We were living a couple of doors down from Ed at that time. The same day that the ransom was paid to the kidnappers, Cheryl and I had left town to drive up to Oregon, and Ed had also left town headed for Mexico City to attend a workshop with Erich Fromm.

The FBI was trying to put the case together and saw these three events happening at once. They were suspicious.

Cheryl and I were headed up to Oregon to visit Elliot and his wife Moose to procure three hundred caps of LSD. I was going to take them back to LA and sell them to enhance the consciousness of that city. The day after Cheryl and I visited their home, the FBI showed up at Elliot's kitchen door—the same kitchen in which we were loading capsules of LSD the day before. When Elliot answered the door, they asked him, "Where is Mark Weiss?"

On our way back from visiting Elliot, we stopped in San Francisco at my brother's house, who was a big-time dope dealer. He wasn't just any dope dealer—he was the best dope dealer around, with shit that would just blow your mind. Cheryl and I stayed there overnight. The next day we were heading back down to LA; we had the three hundred capsules of LSD hidden inside the door of our Volkswagen. The FBI showed up at my brother's house the day after we were there, asking, "Where's Mark?" My brother called me up, asking anxiously, "What the fuck is going on?" We thought the FBI agents might know about the LSD.

When we got back to LA, the FBI gave us a visit. I still had all the caps of acid in the car door and also had a mayonnaise jar full of joints. They had been watching us from a window of one of the apartments across the way and saw the jar of joints. During their visit they took it. At that point, they still didn't know anything about the LSD.

We started having conversations with the FBI and realized they were checking us out to see if we could have been involved in the kidnapping because Ed and we left town the same day as the ransom contact. They even took Cheryl and me out to lunch, and as we were sitting there, they asked me, "Have you ever tried taking LSD?"

"Well, my boss is a researcher, so in terms of research, I've taken LSD," says I.

While we were talking to the Feds, my friend, Gary saw what was going on and got the LSD out of the car door, jumped on his motorcycle, drove off, was followed, and lost the agents that were following him. He ended up burying it in his yard and later proceeded to eat most of it.

Eventually, they became satisfied that we didn't have anything to do with the kidnapping, so they left us alone. So much for my career as a consciousness-enhancing dope dealer. Another example of my financial ineptitude.

Don Briscoe

Don Briscoe was a man caught in a crossfire. He was a business major with a good career ahead of him, and yet he was fully activated in the civil rights movement. He walked a narrow line with genuine concern about how his professors would treat him and the cost he would have to pay if he was identified as a mover and shaker in the movement at the university. He was a man overcoming the fear of being exposed as a troublemaker and struggling to find a place for himself . . . a way of navigating dangerous waters.

A Black man, highly motivated and very articulate, Don was tall, slim, and muscular with short hair and an imposing way of leaning into people that increased his sense of power. He could establish instant rapport with almost anyone he met. He was the color of coffee, with a dash of cream, and he walked with an unapologetic presence. When he spoke, everyone listened. His face conveyed a seriousness coupled with compassion. His eyes seemed to penetrate to the bone.

In his presence, I quickly learned that my heart was in the right place, but my head was behind the times. I was full of the right attitude and nearly inarticulate in language that described the pain and rage emanating from the Black community. The longer we worked together, the more both of us learned that, with effort, we could find a middle way.

In these early stages of the movement in Los Angeles, he was one of the few Black men in the SNCC group.

Although he and I got along personally and were close, the moment we entered into these SNCC planning meetings a competitive energy arose between us. Here we were, two friends, feeling closely aligned emotionally and strategically. However, once we were embedded in this force field of understandings and misunderstandings, it was as if we were caught in a win-lose game with each other. This energy forced us into arguments with no resolution and reactions triggered by darker energies than we realized. The strategies being put forward from the members ranged from "let's negotiate small changes" to "let's arm ourselves and attack the system." Both he and I were trying to find the middle ground but we spoke different languages.

In this maelstrom of highly charged energy, Don and I were thrown together and apart, and meetings often ended in deadlock. At that point, we were only beginning to understand the philosophy of nonviolence, much less how to put it into practice. I felt a great empathy for the anger and rage that emanated from the Black community, and at the same time, intuitively, I knew that nonviolence had to be the key.

OREGON

Oregon Trails

My wife Cheryl and I decided it was time for us to leave Los Angeles, so we packed up our two cats, my upright bass, and everything else that we owned into our Volkswagen and headed north to the University of Oregon. I had been there once before, and I loved it. I thought it was beautiful. When we got up there, we rented a house in a town called Harrisburg, about twenty-some miles outside of Eugene where the university was located. The house was just two blocks from the river and had four bedrooms, but it only cost us sixty-five dollars a month to rent. It had a half-acre of land that we plowed for corn, and we also grew our own little garden.

When we first headed to Oregon, I was completely convinced that all I would have to do was arrive and the sociology department would come running out and say to me, "We've been waiting for you! Come in! We're going to give you a stipend, and we'll give you this and we'll give you that, and you can get a degree here!"

I can't remember exactly how it happened, but that summer I didn't get a stipend or any other goodies. I had put in applications, to no avail. Cheryl and I cut rhubarb and did anything else that we could to make a little money that summer. At the time, I had a little motor scooter I was driving back and forth to save on gas.

Still, we somehow made it work and had some good times. I will never forget the time Cheryl's parents came to visit us in Oregon, and my friend and I took her father fishing. My friend pulled out a joint and offered him a hit. This is what is called in the trade, "bad juju." Her father stormed off behind our house to a garden. Angrily, he walked up to one of the flower trays, pointed to a geranium, and said, "This is marijuana, and I'm going to call the police!"

If he had turned 180 degrees, he would have actually been looking at some marijuana. At any rate, he never followed through on his threat.

Student-Run Class

I began taking classes in the Counseling Psychology department and generally getting involved.

Upon realizing that I represented a dynamic shift in the way counseling could be done, the chairman of the department, Dr. Marty Ackerman, said, "We have an excellent traditional counseling department. We would like for you to stir it up." He had no idea what he was actually asking for or how intense that was going to get. He offered Cheryl and me a double-wide trailer on a five-acre plot of land with a free ride on my path to a master's degree.

Dr. Gordon Dudley, a very nice guy, was my advisor when I was working towards my degree. There was an option for graduate students to teach a class, so I went to him one day and told him that I wanted to teach a student-run class. I titled the class "Marathon Groups, Psychodrama, and the Honesty Revolution." Isn't that bitchin'? That was the way I saw it: that people were using marathon groups and psychodramas to help themselves to be more genuine and real.

I didn't know at the time that these classes were limited to a size of only twelve students. Eighty-five students signed up for my class. I was told I had to cut it down to twelve. Now there were eighty-five enraged graduate students wanting to take my class. The dean of the school was ultimately forced to capitulate because they picketed his office. He ended up letting me open the class to the maximum I felt I could handle which was forty-eight because I had three other leaders. We could do four groups of twelve students. So that left just thirty-seven angry students, but I am just one guy.

My helpers? I knew that I wanted to do these marathon groups and now that I had this enormous class on my hands, I needed help. I called my friends Dave and June Schwartz—who were attending a six-month training program at the Esalen Institute—to help me run things.

The Esalen Institute, located in Big Sur, California, was one of the hippest places in the world. This was during the time when the origination of new psychological thought had abruptly shifted from New York to Los Angeles. Suddenly, in Los Angeles there was a blossoming of new therapeutic approaches like Primal Scream Therapy and Self-actualization.

Dave had given me my first job in psychology sometime around 1968. Actually, at the point of hiring me, he had said, "I may be crazy, but I'm hiring you." I held him in high regard. I invited them to come to Oregon and lead marathon groups with me and Cheryl.

We did four simultaneous marathon groups on the same weekend.

A month later we brought Dave and June back from Esalen and did another set of four student-led marathon groups with the same participants. Cheryl and I monitored the groups throughout the weekend. This time after the groups, we all gathered together in a gymnasium. The purpose was for the members of each of the groups to do a presentation to the other three groups of what kind of changes had occurred in their lives as a result of doing the first marathon.

One group, as a way of expressing what had happened with them, brought in huge rolls of newsprint and colored markers. Everyone in the room was down on the floor painting and writing. They got everybody in the room involved.

Another group walked into the gymnasium wearing overcoats and hats and carrying luggage. They were completely overdressed for the day, the time, and the time of year. They came in and opened up their luggage. Inside were flattened newspapers. They began taking the newspapers out and rolling them into balls. Then they started throwing the balls at the audience, who picked up on it and started hurling them back. During this time, the group began removing all their outerwear and were left in their bathing suits to represent the dropping of masks and defensive postures. Before long, there was a huge, joyous fight—people throwing newspaper balls at each other—and then somebody turned on the music and they started dancing joyously. It was marvelous!

Visions of Chris

Chris was a friend of mine from my time in Los Angeles. He had lived in a small apartment on the beach in Venice, California where we had become buddies and shared our drug experiences with great joy and curiosity. We met at his place to explore some psychedelic territory through the use of mescaline. Within thirty minutes, we were lifting off. Both of us were comfortable with psychedelics and felt safe with each other.

Chris was a social worker and was very relaxed in his attitude. He showed me some yoga positions, and one of my favorites was called the lion pose, a standing position in which you stuck your tongue out exaggeratedly. I was elated to achieve the pose just before I passed out and fell backwards on the cement floor. After a moment or two of disorientation, we spent the next twenty minutes laughing our heads off.

A few years later, when Cheryl and I had settled down in Eugene, Oregon, Chris and his girlfriend, Ellen, decided to visit us. On the day Chris and Ellen were supposed to arrive, we got a call from Ellen saying that on the way up the Ridge Route above Los Angeles, the car struck a boulder on the road and went over a cliff. Ellen reported that Chris had died, but that after his death, he came to her in a vision and gave her directions on how to handle the fact that there were a handful of joints on the floor of the car. He instructed her to tell the police that she had no idea whose drugs they were and to play innocent. These directions came in handy.

The next day, I was driving to a property that Cheryl and I were thinking of purchasing so we could move out of our sixty-foot trailer. Chris appeared to me in the passenger seat, smiling, smoking a joint, and comforting me. I was, in fact comforted at his presence, and glad to know he was doing okay.

Ellen still came up to stay with us for a couple of weeks as soon as she could, and we nurtured her through some of her pain.

Doing Time in Prison

I don't know what it is with me and prisons. Maybe it has to do with the fact that when someone asks me if I can do something odd, weird, or untried, I quickly answer, "Yes." I don't know if that is a character defect or virtue, but it has served me well.

While I was attending graduate school, Cheryl and I had barely been getting by on my stipend when I heard about a three-quarter-time job at Oregon State Prison in Salem. I drove up to Portland for an interview with Dr. Tom Gaddis, the director of the Upward Bound program at the prison. As was my habit, I walked into his office with full confidence that I would get the job.

Tom Gaddis was an interesting and flamboyant character. His claim to fame was that he'd authored a book called The Birdman of Alcatraz, which was later made into a movie starring Burt Lancaster. The two of us hit it off immediately. I described to him the various skills I had, and he hired me on the spot. When he asked me what my job title should be, in a flash I came up with "Group Communication Specialist." It sounded good, and if I were to be asked what it meant, I could improvise confidently.

The Upward Bound program was designed to assist eligible inmates in getting high school and college credits that would prepare them for jobs on the outside. I was going to be part of a team of college teachers preparing selected inmates for college degrees. I was to do both individual and group work with inmates who were preparing to leave prison. I would be conducting pre-release programs to prepare them for the outside world.

One of the programs consisted of groups that focused on re-entry preparation with the inmates. Many of the men in were extremely well-prepared for living life in prison, but not so much for living life in the general community.

The same things that helped them to stay safe in prison—the toughness, the guardedness, the hint of anger just below the surface, the distrust—all worked against them the moment they left prison.

The qualities and overall dangerous appearance of many of these men would almost guarantee that, once released, they would be both harassed by police and shunned by citizens on the outside. The appearance that made them successful in prison became a detriment on the outside. It was my job to help them to prepare for life in the community so that wouldn't happen.

This was a maximum-security prison, and these people—both inmates and guards—meant business. I really couldn't tell who was more afraid of me, the Psychologist, the inmates or the teachers.

I must admit, I liked the adventure of it. I had set my schedule up in such a way that I would only have to drive from Eugene to Salem once a week. I would make the drive every Wednesday, spending two nights inside of the prison and then driving back home on Friday night. On the nights I stayed there, I had my own cell, complete with bed and stark surroundings. The thing that struck me the most was the sound of the metal doors closing behind me. It was chilling.

While there was a psychological impact on me when entering prison for the first time, for the inmates, there was a much greater impact, especially when transitioning back into the world. For example, in prison, it was strictly forbidden for an inmate to touch a telephone because the safety of the prison depended upon them. This was, of course, before the days of cellphones. Phones were the main communication lines between the administration, the guards, and the outside world. A phone was an absolutely critical link there, one that saved lives or prevented tragedy. Such tough restrictions on the phones could cause a long-term impact on these inmates once they were released. Imagine a newly-released prisoner lying on his bed in a motel room when the phone rings, frozen in fear at the dichotomy of wanting to answer the phone and the fear of picking it up.

My relationship with the other staff members in our Upward Bound program was somewhat strained. The academic professors had a low regard for psychology, a disdain, even, but every time we interviewed potential inmates for our program, they insisted that I be there.

My relationship with the inmates seemed to come naturally. There was one particular inmate that stands out in my memory who had spent fifteen years in the maximum-security prison in Joliet, Illinois and was now doing an additional five years here with us. He was working on his master's degree in anthropology. He was stocky with red hair and a menacing countenance. He walked like a gorilla and could easily have frightened people on the street. I used video feedback to show him his visual impact and to help him revise the way he communicated with people. By the time he was ready to leave the program, he had become gentler, more open, and less fearsome.

When you work in a prison, "getting conned" is the way you earn your stripes. Whereas I had eight hours out of the day to work with the inmates, they had twenty-four hours to figure out how to con me. I never took it personally—it was just a part of the culture.

The most intense experience I had being conned was with a guy named Lucky. Lucky was glib, bright, and intensely interested in group work. I took him under my wing and taught him to be a therapist, showing him the finer points of group processes and teaching him how to level with people. Months later, I discovered that he was loan-sharking and selling drugs right under my nose with no regard for the connection we had been building—a connection that I considered to be warm and valuable. He had been dealing drugs the entire time.

When I confronted him, he openly admitted to what he had been doing and asserted that it served him financially. In my situation, if I had blown the whistle on him, it would have destroyed all the rapport we had been building as a group, so I decided to let it slide.

The Prison Riot

One Saturday afternoon during a staff meeting with Tom Gaddis in Portland, I suggested conducting a marathon group for twelve of the inmates in our program. After I explained the process and told him about the origins at Camarillo State Hospital in California with institutionalized juvenile delinquents, he approved my request.

At seven o'clock, twelve inmates and I entered one of our fourth-floor classrooms to begin. I had already explained to them that there would be no educational content and that the only requirement was that we speak honestly to one another as adults. Since a number of the inmates had known me for an extended period of time, we were quickly able to move into a level of honest communication.

Some of the inmates opened up and talked about their goals and plans for the future while others remained reticent and distrusting. We ended around midnight and came back together at nine in the morning on Saturday.

Around noon, as I was walking around the room, I looked out the window and saw an inmate knocking down a guard. My first thought was: This is bad. And then it got worse. I looked around and saw other guards being knocked down and attacked. I would say that it brought the marathon to an end.

Now, we had a whole new set of problems. On our floor, there were only two staff people, me and one of the professors. We could hear shouting and we began to smell smoke. The inmates who were rioting had set fire to the first and second floors. It occurred to me that we should lock the iron door to the floor that we were on for our protection. That way, when the inmates who were rioting came to the fourth floor, these twelve inmates could tell them that they couldn't find the keys. We also put paper in the waste cans and set them on fire to give the impression to the other inmates that our floor was on fire too. This kept the rioters from trying to break in.

Abruptly, my role had shifted. I realized that I was utterly calm. I sat down and began counseling the inmates on the fourth floor. They wanted me to know that if these rioters broke in, they couldn't defend me because they had to live with the consequences, which could be very dangerous for them. Out of some deep well of calm and compassion, I let them know that I understood, that it was okay, and that I would be fine. If I were to die in this situation, this was exactly where I wanted to be, so there was nothing for me to fear.

After a few hours of continuous rioting, we saw a fire truck outside. It had a hook and ladder that extended across the wall of the prison, all the way to the fourth-floor window. A fireman climbed up the ladder with an acetylene torch and cut the bars from the window. Then, all of us—inmates and staff members—climbed to safety, four stories down to a spot outside the wall of the prison.

In some kind of bizarre coincidence, Cheryl had been invited to take a ride in a small plane that same day and was flying over the prison as it was happening, seeing the smoke, but having no idea what it was or that I was there.

The Master's Exam

At the University, hired at the same time as I, was another guy named Merv Wingard. Merv and his wife, Judy, technically lived in two places: in Washington, somewhere up in the mountains during the summer doing tower observations, looking for fires, and in Tucson, Arizona during the winter. They lived in a development for intellectuals. They had streets there with names like Galileo Street where they had discussion groups and had string quartets come out and play.

Merv and I formed a group of about six graduate students, and we went to the faculty to ask them to give us nine hours and $500 apiece per semester to educate ourselves. They knew my work and so they agreed.

We started conducting psychodramas and marathon groups. Throughout that semester, if we wanted to learn about some particular subject, we would go to the professors and interview them or have lunch with them. In order to get our credit hours and money, we were obligated to do a presentation for the graduate school students at the end of the semester about what we had learned.

At this point, everything was more or less copacetic until it came time for the comprehensive exam. In the comprehensive exam, we were asked a certain number of questions. Everyone had a yellow legal pad of paper and a pen. When the proctor asked a question, we would write it down and answer it. There were fifteen or twenty people in the room, and everyone was ready for the timed test.

I was wearing tall moccasin boots and wide-leg red corduroy pants on which Cheryl had put red velvet flares. I was bald with a bushy red beard. As if walking in dressed like that wasn't bad enough, I also didn't have a yellow pad. Instead, I had great big sheets of white paper and brightly-colored marking pens. I was drawing all kinds of things on my paper, which was just my process of thinking. It was odd, but then again, they knew I was odd.

Although on this day I was having very intense arthritis pain, I was still loving what I was doing and could have done it all day. The woman who was the secretary to the dean was acting as the proctor for the test, and she announced that we only had five more minutes until time would be up. That was when — in my pain and anger — I scrawled across the page a venomous written tirade sharp enough to cut. I am fairly certain that the scathing words I chose to write *might* have come to me from all the prison work I had been doing. My language had become *so* much more colorful over the time I spent there.

Naturally, the proctor saw the difference between my exam and everyone else's, so she decided to read it. She then carried it directly to the dean. The dean read it and called a meeting of the faculty in which he insisted that they unanimously kick me out of the school.

The political strategy working here was that if anyone stood up for me, they would have to go against the entire department faculty and dean and would risk losing their job. This included my advisor, whom I really loved and who really loved me. His hands were tied. I went to the chairman of the department, who was also unable to do anything to help my situation.

I was told that I had no way out. I had straight A's in all of my classes, but here I was, facing expulsion.

I had recently started studying yoga to help me with my arthritis. The teacher's name was Dr. Kundu, and he was very familiar with the work of Gandhi and with non-violent resistance. When I told Dr. Kundu what was going on with my degree and told him that I wasn't sure what to do, he told me to hold a sit-in.

Cheryl and I went to the counseling center where they had a large group room, and we took a seat next to each other. By this time, the Students for a Democratic Society (SDS) had heard what was going on, and they had also shown up in the cafeteria with sleeping bags ready to sit in. Then the Black Graduate Students' Organization told me, "We're going to sit in with you too, because if they can do this to you, then they can do this to us."

A woman walked into the room and said to us, "I'm sorry, but you're going to have to leave, because we have a counseling group coming in." I looked her dead in the eye and told her that I was going to sit here until I die.

At this point, even more students had come in and were sitting around. We were all really getting into it. After a couple of hours, the president of the university finally heard about it and called me on a phone which someone brought me. The president, who later became Secretary of Health, Education, and Welfare of the United States said, "If you are willing to call off this sit-in, I'll call an emergency meeting of faculty and students, and we'll form a faculty-student committee to take this under advisement."

"All right," I said. "You're the president."

The next morning, everyone was pretty grumpy. By eight o'clock, the students and faculty had gathered in the large group room. We had formed the first student-faculty grievance committee in the history of the school. In the meantime, the faculty had held a meeting on their own. They had completely packed the student-faculty committee with their people, so again, they essentially fucked me. I was ready to go back and start the sit-in all over again. They already knew that they were stuck in a position where they couldn't go against the other faculty members.

There was a guy there named Dr. James Lowe who was head of an Upward Bound program that had been working with and teaching children who came from a life of poverty. He was the first one other than my advisor who actually looked at my records and transcripts. He turned to the crowd and announced, "This guy has all the requirements necessary to get a degree in Human Development."

The committee decided that they would allow me to retake my comprehensive exam in the field of Human Development. I showed up for the exam this time with a yellow pad and a pencil. I took the test and passed it, and I graduated with a master's degree in human development.

Dr. Kundu

Throughout my time at the University of Oregon, Cheryl and I had been eating a macrobiotic diet, which was centered on brown rice and vegetables. I was probably in the best shape I had been in since my illness in 1961, and I credit my healthy state at the time for allowing me to safely descend the ladder at the prison riot.

I was advised to quit the macrobiotic diet by Dr. Kundu, who had been our yoga teacher. My wife had taken me to meet him when my arthritis had gotten really bad. He took one look at me and said, "Get off of this macrobiotic stuff." I was in such an enormous amount of pain at the time, I would have done just about anything. I thought to myself, if this guy can help me, I'll do it.

The next thing I knew, he was instructing us on what to do and what to eat, so I began cooking and eating Indian food, which in hindsight, was probably not a very good idea. Cheryl started to take a real dislike to him. She was a whole lot smarter than I was, but in my defense, I was in a whole lot of pain.

Dr. Kundu had just gotten his PhD in physical education and sent out all kinds of résumés, and he had managed to land a job at Benedict College, an historically Black college, in Colombia, South Carolina. At the time, I had been going around recruiting other graduate students to be his students and there were about four of us altogether. When Cheryl heard about South Carolina and realized that I would follow Dr. Kundu, she decided that she was bailing on our relationship. She said that she wasn't going to South Carolina or anywhere else with that guy! I was just thinking if he could help me with the pain, I had to do this.

Because I'd gone through so much severe pain in my life, at this point I had already made the decision that I was not going to father any biological children. I felt that it would just be too dangerous. My brother had gotten arthritis, I had arthritis—I just didn't want to pass those genes along. I'm not even sure exactly how accurate genetic testing was back then, but at any rate, my mind was made up.

When Cheryl and I got married, we had already agreed that we were not going to have children. Somewhere along the line, Cheryl had changed her mind about that and she stopped taking the pill. I was feeling betrayed, frustrated, and angry, so I basically let our sex life go to hell. Not to mention that there was already a sense of distance between us while we had been doing all the marathon groups, and the distance continued to grow.

Looking back, I know now how many stupid things I did and I can see all of the things that I should have done differently, but at that time, I just didn't realize it. In one of her marathon groups Cheryl ended up meeting a young guy who was into yoga. She connected with him, so it ultimately turned out okay.

COLUMBIA, SOUTH CAROLINA

Goodbye, Cheryl.

I drove to Columbia, and after getting established, I drove back to Oregon for one last conversation with Cheryl, in which I asked her to come with me. I didn't realize that—as we were in the front having our discussion—her new boyfriend was in the back of our trailer. I wouldn't learn of this until later when Cheryl and her boyfriend stopped in San Francisco at my brother's house. They were on their way to LA and asked him if he would put them up for the night. My brother, in an act that I would never have predicted, refused their request in honor of my feelings.

After talking with Cheryl, it became clear that we weren't going to work things out and we ultimately ended up getting a divorce. That would be the last time I heard from her for the next decade.

At one time or another, she actually was in South Carolina at the same time I was. She had gone to New York and was studying with Sachidananda—one of the gurus. At some point in time, I had written her a letter and a poem and sent it to her parents because I didn't know where she was living. Her parents forwarded it to her and we reconnected. By then, she had gone through a lot of changes herself and was married with a son.

Looking back now, I think Cheryl was absolutely right in her evaluation of Dr. Kundu as being overly controlling, vindictive, and narcissistic.

"Go, Cocks, Go!"

As I was driving into Columbia for the first time, I saw a huge billboard that said "Go, Cocks, Go!" Later, I would learn that the Gamecocks were actually the basketball team of USC, but at the moment I saw that billboard, I knew that I was in for it.

Once I arrived in Colombia, I decided to apply for the PhD program in Counselor Education. After my experiences in Oregon as a highly visible radical, I decided to play things very close to the vest. I wore white shirts and ties and did my best to stay out of the limelight. My experience in Mississippi had taught me a little something about the narrow scope of acceptable thought.

When I entered the PhD program, I realized that many of the professors had never left college. They had gone from degree to degree, earning their PhD but never actually having their feet on the street. When they recognized the depth and variation in my background, there were two primary responses: curiosity and abject fear.

ANOTHER SECESSION

What a terrible confusion!
South Carolina's honor
Hanging in the balance
Of a conversation on counselling
In a room that could have been better
In a school preparing blind people
To teach the lame.

Why is it so necessary for you

To defend a large ugliness
With a tiny truth? The world,
My God, the world is whimpering
In its loneliness; that terrible loneliness.

What a luxury is this sad,
Empty holding on (I must tell you
That I've experienced with my eyes
And my nerves that crucifixion
Of children we call school)
And walking among the ruins
Of teachers once starstruck
And now hope-less, dead,
And counselors too cynical for
Feeling, searching for a fuse
To ignite, a pulse to quicken
An eye to brighten—oh laughter!
Laughter is a remedy and a release
And an opening of your lungs
And crying out—a mutual seeing.

⸻

Dr. Don McKenzie was the curious professor. He wanted to become my advisor because he wanted to learn more about my therapeutic approach. I was being advised at the time by the chairman of the department, Dr. Tom Sweeny. Tom—being the consummate academe citizen that he was—maintained his emotional distance. I decided that I needed to switch from Sweeny to McKenzie, so I went to Dr. Kundu and asked him for advice on how to do it. He said, "In India during the British occupation, one could not just advise an Englishman. One had to 'oil' them."

"Oiling" was the act of flattering your English boss and convincing him that your idea was actually his idea. I went directly to Dr. Sweeny and told him how valuable his help had been, how much I had learned from him, and what a great support he had been. None of these things was particularly true. I then told him that Don McKenzie was interested in studying some of my approaches and asked if it would be okay if I made him my primary advisor. Dr. Sweeny gave a noticeable sigh of relief. Don McKenzie became my teacher, my student, and my friend. I had dinner with his family many times and we spent a lot of time just talking and playing music.

In order to allow me the time to finish my doctoral program, I needed a job that was three-quarter-time. By chance, that was exactly what I found. My first job there was at the State Department of Vocational Rehabilitation focusing on research and training. I was hired by the director, Dr. Chandler, who was an older man with severe scoliosis, so he was permanently bent over. He hired me and another graduate student, Barry Reichstein, who was from New York.

As I read the lay of the land, I realized that our boss preferred having two three-quarter-time employees, as there was less likelihood of us taking his job. From the very beginning of my work with him, it became clear that he was not interested in our productivity. He almost never gave us assignments and was perfectly okay with me working on my PhD at the office. For me, it was a great invitation to use my time to work on my dissertation.

Barry, on the other hand, became more and more frustrated with the idea that he was being paid for a job that involved no meaningful work. His anxiety and frustration ultimately led him to quit both the job and graduate school and to go back to New York.

I managed to convince Dr. Chandler to purchase $6,000 worth of video equipment that had a dual purpose. I was touting it as a great asset to the training department—one that I could use for training vocational rehabilitation counselors—but being the clever boy that I was, I also used it to conduct all the research for my dissertation. In actuality, I used it much more for my dissertation than I did for training.

I was interested in the effects of videotape feedback with mixed racial groups. The title of my dissertation was "The Effects of Videotape Focused Feedback on Facilitative Genuineness in Interracial Encounters," which was almost as long as the dissertation itself.

The kinds of things I was interested in studying and writing my dissertation on had to do with interracial encounters and how people dealt with one another. I had first been introduced to the idea of videotaped feedback—as well as the idea of a marathon group—by Dr. Fred Stoller. Fred had been experimenting with a technique he called "Videotape-focused feedback." It was a group process in which participants were videotaped for the purpose of later giving them feedback. In particular, it showed them the discrepancies between their intentions and how they actually came across to others.

The purpose of the videotaped feedback was to help people to grasp the effects of their negative self-talk and to then change it into positive self-talk. The focus was almost entirely on how people presented themselves. The moment I saw and experienced the process, I knew there was something much deeper to be found in Fred's work. I was already aware of the immense power of both negative and positive self-talk in people's lives, and I was now seeing a doorway opening that would allow therapists to directly access negative self-talk. This would allow them to immediately assist their patients in revising and improving their self-language. This was the approach that I decided to test in my dissertation.

To test the effect of the videotaped feedback, I set up a room behind a one-way mirror. I had groups of black people and white people meeting on a regular basis. I split the subjects into two groups—both being videotaped with one group getting feedback and one without feedback. I had three trained observers watching these groups and grading them on facilitative genuineness—in other words, people who were being real and trying to help as opposed to those who were full of bullshit.

I would then share the videotapes with the participants in one group and give them feedback. Then both groups met and were observed again and were rated on whether there was a significant change in their level of facilitative genuineness.

For each subject, the scores of the three observers were compared. If the scores they received from all three observers were similar, they were found to be genuine. Ultimately, I was able to demonstrate that giving people video feedback increased their sense of self-awareness and aided in breaking down the barriers to being helpfully genuine.

Becoming a Sports Aficionado

While living in Columbia South Carolina and working for the Department of Vocational Rehabilitation in the Research and

Training Department, all the people I worked with were deeply into sports, and around the time of the World Series, it was even more intensified.

One day that season, I was driving to work knowing that we had a meeting with the director of our organization, a 75-year-old man who, on his 75th birthday was given a shotgun. Now, I always arrived on time for these meetings, but the director didn't. This meant sitting around shooting the shit with everyone else until he got there, in this case about the World Series. As I drove to work, I turned on the radio and heard a brief commentary about the final game of the series. The commentator said "I think this is the best year McDougall has ever had," and I turned off the radio.

As I settled in to wait for the director—I'd had a few nightmares of the doddering director coming into the room with his new shotgun and blowing us all away. The discussion began. It was the equivalent of bar talk, in which anyone that had a beer in their hand could provide astute commentary. As the comments flowed around the room, I found my opening.

"This is the best year McDougall has ever had," I piped in. Everyone nodded in approval.

Manning Correctional Institute

A Desegregation Center was housed at the University as a part of the Title I Program. This program was aimed at directing attention to preschool and elementary education, as well as the issue of desegregation in the schools. My experiences in Mississippi and Watts made me a prime candidate for evaluating public schools all over South Carolina and assisting them in dealing with the structural and emotional problems of integration. So, I joined the center and was traveling around with them as a group facilitator. We were trying to help black and white teachers and faculty adjust to the new laws, but we were encountering a great deal of resistance—mostly from the administrators.

We were trying to open dialogue among educators, teachers, PTA organizations and administrators dealing with desegregation. Many of these teachers had never had to talk to black people and now were being forced into it. Most commonly, we encountered groups of teachers—mostly female—that were complaining about authoritarian white school principals.

Ultimately, we were hampered by diversions such as false reports and bogus evaluations trumped up by the administrators to show "data" that stated that things were proceeding better than they actually were. I enjoyed the work, but was frustrated by our lack of impact. Thankfully, there would be other opportunities.

As part of my educational program, I was invited by Dr. Wilhelm Mayer to work part-time as a group facilitator at Manning Correctional Institute, a minimum-security institution in South Carolina. Dr. Mayer was interested in applying the marathon group concept to the corrections system, and he had come up with a brilliant idea for training inmates to help young offenders in the juvenile justice system.

One of the most common desires expressed by adult offenders was, "If only I could talk to these young kids in trouble to steer them away from the mistakes I made." Dr. Mayer took this statement literally and formed a coalition between Manning Correctional Institute and the juvenile detention center called Youth Authority, which was not far from the prison.

Dr. Mayer's idea was to bring selected inmates to an empty cell block there and have them set up offices with desks and chairs where they could do direct counseling with these troubled kids who were living there. When we announced the program in the prison, over eighty inmates volunteered.

Our next task was to devise a selection process that would sort out inmates who were mature enough and who were on a rehabilitative path. In discussions with Dr. Mayer, I suggested that one of the criteria would be the successful completion of a weekend marathon group. He and a number of other professors had already attended groups I had run. He was impressed with the growth potential and ability to achieve authentic connection.

We immediately implemented the program and began selecting inmates for the marathon group and young people to participate in the counseling program. A date was set for the weekend marathon. I was to conduct the event, and Dr. Mayer would join.

I set up the marathon to start on a Friday evening. I asked what the unspoken rules of prison were. I was told that you never, ever said anything negative about a man's mother. It did not matter how much the inmate hated his mother. He might say his mother was a hateful drug addict bitch, but if you made a comment about her, you were dead. Noted.

From the beginning of that session, I laid out a scenario for the participants that involved what is called "the dozens." It's a game, sometimes deadly, in which men will colorfully demean your physical condition, or your family, even your mother.

I told the inmate counselors that at the moment they felt they were most helpful to a young offender, that offender was going to say something about their mother, and it was their responsibility to not be reactive to it.

I began playing the dozens in the marathon group on Saturday afternoon, talking about some things I knew about an inmate's mother. Dixie, the inmate involved and one of the inmate counselors, became incensed and came running across the room at me with his fist raised. I think Dr. Mayer wet his pants. The room was electric.

Intuitively, I knew that becoming vulnerable was the key to dealing with this kind of attack. While he was yelling at me and shaking his fist in my face, I instinctively leaned back into my chair and opened my legs into a very vulnerable position. I reached out and put my hand around his fist and said, "We can deal with this." He immediately calmed down and everyone in the room breathed a sigh of relief. I knew, inside, that if he could deal with this and not be destructive, he was qualified for the program. We watched him become aware of his rage and regulate it by himself.

A large man in the group revealed to us that he was a "banker" in the prison. People borrowed money from him at exorbitant rates of interest, and he was big and strong enough to do his own collections. Our fundamental negotiation was that as long as he held his position, he would be at odds with the goal of our program. Throughout the marathon, he struggled with the idea that he would lose his position as an inmate counselor, something he believed in, if he didn't let go of his banker role. By the end of the weekend, he had committed himself to changing his role at the prison in exchange for membership in our counselor group.

The program was quite successful. The juvenile offenders understood clearly that these inmate counselors had done everything they were doing and more and took counsel from these older men. I took with me the satisfaction of knowing that I had helped the inmates empower themselves so that they could help the youth offenders. I left the inmate counselling program to complete my approaching dissertation.

PhD—Threatening Another Sit-in

My dissertation was successful other than one little glitch. The dean had assigned a professor to be his representative on the committee charged with the acceptance of my dissertation. The University of South Carolina was in a very segregated area in 1970, and the problem with the guy he put on my committee was that he was a racist who made money on the side by going around to high schools in South Carolina to help them to avoid desegregation.

My PhD had the words "Interracial Encounters" in it. When that man saw those words in my title, he refused to sign it.

I had tried so hard to conform. I had been wearing a white shirt and even a tie every day. I had a nice, short haircut, was handling various professors with aplomb, and was doing quite well. At this point, my esteemed advisor, Don McKenzie, stepped in and confronted the professor, asking for a written list of his objections to my dissertation. Everything the guy put down was complete and total bullshit. The list he gave contained fourteen criticisms, of which not a single one was true.

Ever the inventive, I decided upon my own course of action. I sought out the biggest blabbermouth among the students in our department and said to her, "My parents are coming here in January for my graduation. If this professor doesn't sign my dissertation, I will fill the dean's office with protestors from now until the end of next year. He will not get any work done." Then I waited.

Within thirty minutes, I got an urgent message from the dean's office that he wanted to see me immediately. I went into his office very calmly. As I was walked into his office, he looked up at me and said, "You're being an ass!"

I looked right back at him and replied, "I'm the one getting fucked!"

Clearly, he knew that I meant business, and within ten minutes, he agreed to sign my dissertation himself. My parents attended my graduation that January.

It was a sunny day in Mudville.

Here is a poem I submitted to be read at the graduation ceremony. I was told that the committee did not want to use exhortative poetry. Alas, it was not read, but it was my first published poem.

GRADUATION

(On the event of receiving my PhD at the University of South Carolina—the intellectual home of racism. Published in New Voices in Education.)

I

I am singing today,
    and crying
The eyes and faces of those
    within me
Shine and shine

not from this empty paper
But from those whose minds
        demand my honesty
In this moment I am whole

II

Commencement is a little late
        I commenced in Mississippi
And entered a path surrounded by death
And a deeper love than
        television ever considered
I had to discover how alone I was
I wandered through my fears
        touching people's hearts
Crying out "come to your true self"
Waiting to come to my own true self
And I am older now

III

If I had your collective consciousness
        spread across my eyes
The light would shine through in places
        where you are most brave
My classmates, brothers and sister of my time,
        will you break the circle of lies?
I reside in a corner of your heart
        where truth resides
Where the strength is found
        for the frightening facing of yourself
Emptiness frightens us most
        and the singing which is

always in the universe

IV

What a larger universe it seems
Expanding as a model for my mind
        fighting down the urge
          to crawl into my fears
Glancing sideways at my elders -
They are trying to run the world like
         a farm or a candy store
         balancing the books
Prepared to fight the deer and the bear
Or to kill quite easily the terrible other
         a deeper meaning is here
         its crystal clarity vibrates
A terrible alarm clock shouting
"My God, what are we doing?"
         that penetrating panic
         that wakes us momentarily.
Night ascends, assails the mountains
And man's deepest urge to freedom pulses

V

What a strain - to be something
         other than ourselves
Powerless to draw upon our
         original energies
Manufacturing love and youth
         and plastic maturity.
I am at the end of the educational tunnel
         the Ph.D., the final whip

The award for not saying what I meant,
    making a habit of it
O God, was it worth it? I have tried
    to stay alive
To breathe the universe in and out
    and dance and shout
And sit quietly and save my strength
    I have to use it now
Use it for the purpose that is music's purpose -
    waking men's souls.
John Coltrane! You were black
    and your black music
(with Monk and Miles and Duke)
    and the terrible angry sweetness
That helped me through my minor
    but necessary first death.
It took my pain to help me see the
    beauty in your pain
That impossible anguish and serene
    awareness you lived daily.
What an awful emptiness I sense
    in my white brothers.

VII

Buckminster Fuller said to me,
    "What an insanity,
That thirty-five growing human minds
    would appear at the same place
In time, and be interested in Italian Geography."
We have been railroaded down a long line
    of straight-backed chairs

Of straight-backed teachers (with one or two
        who might have loved us
Had they been able to touch us
        or even speak the truth).
I'd slip away, were I to do it again.
        slip away at every moment
And try to understand the ocean
        and the sunrise.
The birds know and rise swiftly
        in anticipation
While I learned to filter it through
        my reading glasses
Psychology, the high church of modern man
        a complex catalogue of sins
In boxes and cans and prizes for self deception
        positively reinforced.
Have you noticed that there are fewer
        normal people?
The definition of normal keeps narrowing
        as we search for sinners
Enemies of the state - disadvantaged, poor,
        deprived, mentally ill
Handicapped, convicts, blacks, Indians,
        underachievers, gifted,
Artists, musicians, poets, unwed mothers,
        certain students -
We'll ferret them out and correct them
        and write their story in video
And admire their life-like qualities
        We're resurrecting Johnny Cash
One hundred years too late, and the men
        whose music shines

Like drops of pain across our tired eyes
        they are black and frightening,
They hold the key to freedom
        they die unknown to us.
We are always startled when we
        encounter them
Martin Buber told me I must
        practice directness
Even if I were the only man on earth
        who did it
And not depart from it until scoffers
        are struck with fear
And hear in my voice the voice
        of their own suppressed longing.

VIII

I guess (I really know) I'm tired
        of all the artificial flowers
Tired of deadening my senses so others
        might indulge in lies.
I know that you know what's happening
        you avert your eyes from mine
Skillfully evade your own feelings
Avoiding -
        evoking the various gods who populate
            the locker room and tavern
                the small minded chatter
                    of worthless, endless
                        meetings
I'm sick and tired of being told
        to overlook the children's eyes

To see your fear-built white man's
      ego flash I.Q.
Vanity -
      killing slowly (and smiling)
         a child's will to dream
            and all the while in pulpits
               begging his
                  forgiveness

It must come to an end
It must come to an end
      or commence (to begin
         the face of mankind shining
            in your face) the world
               is me and you
                  you know
                     the truth

Act! The time is growing late
      hate oozes in the door
         unhinged, the mind of man
            requires that we act -
               a touch is the
                  commencement of
                    our courage

There is in me a fierce hope
I have seen your face alive for moments
      alive your heart bursting
         eyes clear unburdened
         by lies
Your eyes, your secret is in my eyes
      when you no longer fear
         your eyes or mine
            penetrating to the heart

or the tears that rise
you are free
Stoned! Getting stoned is how we
cut off ourselves from ourselves
my foot was in that sweet grave
my aliveness and the love
of people and my hope
released me

You've got to function to do good,
your heart must be pure
or it always turns sour
always whimpers in the end
"I tried, don't you know?
I tried."
Your eyes must be clear, unfogged
the strength emerges from your roots
commitment to the longest song
the hardest tune
the truth

IX

The American dream is written daily
in beer cans and burned-out cars
and people burned out
in the insane drive
for things
The soul of America - it is not a political
argument
It is not a case of law or differing

educational theory
The heart knows
my heart knows you
And love is not a weaving body selling
cigarettes and lies.
Doing right, your body and your mind
tell you
Listen! Listen to the pulse, the blood,
your own true nature
You were once a child
now you are stepping through
a velvet curtain into the
face of God
There are no lies here, only the momentary
panic, the pain, the struggle,
the joy and, peace.

After receiving my doctorate I got a job at Allen University, a Black college. Dr. Kundu was working at Benedict College across the street. I was teaching psychology and found it frustrating because many of the students believed that the walk on the moon was fabricated because their parents believed that and had told them so.

There was, at the university, a super-teacher, a woman who taught Spanish. I invited her to come over to Allen University and use her best teaching skills to help me awaken the students to a new kind of learning curve. We used repetition, storytelling and games. None of which had any effect on improving test scores. The experiment failed and I felt very frustrated. There were only so many strategies I could use without stepping across some kind of boundary.

Unexpectedly, I was offered an alternate position in the university as the director of an early childhood learning center. The children were behaving in a chaotic way as if they had no awareness of the rules of the game. I immediately saw that what these children needed was a program based on behavior modification. I purchased aprons with pockets in them for all of the teachers and instructed them that any time they saw a child behaving properly that they pop an M&M in their mouth. Within the first day or two the kids realized that if they wanted an M&M, they would have to demonstrate certain kinds of behavior. Within a week these kids were focused on the kinds of behaviors we wanted them to show. Immediately I was seen as some sort of savior. The classrooms quieted down, civil interchange became the norm and teaching was possible.

The End of the Kundu Era

Throughout my time in South Carolina, I became very involved in the teachings of Dr. Kundu. The Hindu philosophy was called Vedanta. Dr. Kundu had introduced me to the work of two very famous gurus: Ramakrishna and his disciple, Swami Vivekananda. Almost every weekend, I would drive up to Spartanburg, and Merv, Judy, and Ron—the students who had followed him to South Carolina when I did—and Dr. and Mrs. Kundu and I would drive to experience natural settings— waterfalls, the woods, etcetera. I really developed a deep appreciation for nature, especially having come from New York City.

After I had received my doctorate we travelled throughout Oregon, the Carolinas, Florida, and India. We spent six weeks travelling from Calcutta to Benares, Agra, Delhi, and Bombay. I prepared and cooked Indian food for our journeys with Mrs. Kundu and I took direction from Dr. Kundu in terms of hygiene, yoga, and daily advice.

In addition to nurturing my spiritual side, I was also on a mission to enrich my professional side. After reading the book Parent Effectiveness Training, I immediately saw its value for parents learning to negotiate with their children. Its Win/Win approach seemed valuable. It was based on the work of Carl Rogers, an eminent psychologist and writer. I knew that I wanted to be a part of the program which trained trainers to train parents on communication skills.

I flew out to Pasadena in Southern California and walked into the office of Effectiveness Training Associates unannounced and asked to see Dr. Thomas Gordon, the author of the book and president of the company. He greeted me at the door to his office.

I introduced myself, "I'm Mark Weiss, and I am your regional associate for Georgia and South Carolina."

He seemed quite startled but also intrigued. We spent two hours together talking about the program, and I left his office as the regional associate for Parent Effectiveness Training in Georgia and South Carolina.

When I returned from California, I immediately began teaching and training instructors. I'm not sure where my supreme confidence came from, other than that my attention was real and focused. I knew this was what I should be doing.

Dr. Kundu had taken an interest in my work and insisted that I raise my rates. In hindsight, there couldn't have been a worse business decision. I was only just getting started and this choice alienated many of my instructors. As I watched my business diminish, Tom Gordon came from California and offered to pay me $3,000 to give up my title as regional associate. To add insult to injury, Dr. Kundu insisted that half of that money should go to him. This was the beginning of the end of my work with him.

This ending coincided with my having an affair with a married woman and getting caught by one of Dr. Kundu's students. One day, she had left a note on my door. It didn't say much of anything—just "I missed you." When another one of Dr. Kundu's students saw it, she showed it to Dr. Kundu. The next time I saw him in Spartanburg, he asked me to reveal everything that had gone on. As long as he was my teacher, I was bound to tell him the truth. He immediately demanded that I move to Spartanburg, South Carolina, where he resided.

I was torn between my obligations to the University and my obligations to Dr. Kundu. I chose Dr. Kundu and immediately submitted my resignation at Allen University and said my goodbye to my girlfriend. I felt ashamed and humiliated, but I was compelled to follow Dr. Kundu's direction. For some reason I still believed that he could help in my recovery from crippling arthritis, while in reality I was ignoring the fact that my condition had not improved.

Almost immediately after the move, I got a position working in Greer, South Carolina for a research group from Columbia University in New York.

Before long, I finally came to the realization that I was not cut out to be anyone's disciple, and I told Dr. Kundu I was leaving. I remember vividly being in his apartment with three of his students that I had recruited. He essentially put a curse on me, telling me that people who left him had bad things happen to them. He then took the check for $1,500 that he owed me and threw it on the floor. It was humiliating and shocking. But it was the end of Skim Scam, the Rubber Man.

SKIM SCAM THE RUBBER MAN

Skim Scam the rubber man
  Stretches to infinity
Everything to
  Everyone
    yet
Only lonely in his
  Darkened self
The razor sharp
  Performance of
    The perfect act.

As I left his apartment, I saw Mrs. Kundu, who had always treated me with gentle care. I said farewell to her with tears streaming down my face. The end to my relationship with Dr. Kundu was brutal. There was something strangely familiar about this event. Years later, I realized that it duplicated the same kind of bitter experience I'd had with my father when I left home for San Francisco. Ten years later, Merv and Judy would try to leave him, and he would do the same thing to them.

In addition to the job with Columbia University, I had also been hired by the Air Force to speak on family mental health to a large group of Air Force personnel at a retreat owned by Billy Graham in the Blue Ridge Mountains. This was where I met Gina, who would become my second wife. She was there with her parents, who were there for marriage enhancement. Gina was twelve years younger than I and relatively naïve.

I was afloat. I was still rebounding with shock at the way my relationship with my teacher had deteriorated, and I couldn't imagine a worse time to be entering into a new relationship.

It was the equivalent of breaking up with a domineering, controlling partner or ending a marriage and being on the rebound. At that point, my spiritual life was on hiatus—in a state of limbo. I was in a dissociated trance. As was my style, I hooked up with Gina anyway.

I had convinced Gina to come with me to Boone, North Carolina where my best friend, Bob Jones, lived. I thought that his soul-enhancing effect on me would help me work through my shock.

I'm sure that with our age difference, I overwhelmed Gina. In the blindness of my state, I had no real ability to discriminate between healthy and unhealthy relationship behaviors. I was reeling.

After a number of visits to her parents' home, where I could display my socially sanctioned wares such as having a doctorate, working with the Air Force, and working for a university, I prematurely took the plunge and proposed to Gina. We scheduled a wedding in Minot, North Dakota, at the Air Force base where Gina had been born.

My parents and my uncle Nate came to the wedding, as did Gina's parents. I'd borrowed a bass fiddle for my father to play, and Uncle Nate brought his tenor saxophone. I flew in a wonderful pianist by the name of Dave Robertson, who had worked with me at the Unitarian church in Los Angeles. He improvised the music for the wedding, and afterward, we played some jazz.

ATLANTA, GEORGIA

Going in Circles

Gina and I drove to Atlanta. On the way there, we went through a toll booth to get on the interstate, which circled the perimeter of Baltimore. I said hello to the woman at the toll booth and drove merrily on my way. After forty-five minutes of driving, we pulled up to another toll booth and the same woman was there. I had literally driven in a big circle around Baltimore and ended up in the exact same place. The symbolism of this event did not register with me at the time. Later, I realized that going around in circles may have accurately described my marriage.

The Practice

Gina and I moved to Atlanta and got an apartment on the outskirts of town. I had a series of jobs there, beginning with one at the Georgia State Department of Education, Research, and Evaluation.

I was hired to monitor the effectiveness of funding for desegregation in Georgia's education system. I traveled around the state meeting with teachers and administrators. I soon came to realize that funds which were supposed to go to Title I educational programs were being used instead for building gymnasiums.

I worked there for exactly five months and twenty-nine days and was fired on the last day of my six-month probationary period. I had actually been thinking of going home that day, and if I had, I would have been unavailable for firing and would have made it through the probationary period.

In my time working there, I had become very depressed witnessing how unscrupulous their practices were, and they had caught on to the fact that I had begun documenting the discrepancies, so they took all those functions away from me and left me with only one task—to design the cover for the falsified evaluation reports. On this task, I did an excellent job, and I left with a bang. Well, actually more of a whimper.

I applied for a job as a clinical staff member for a communications training program. At the end of the interview, I was asked to teach a demonstration class so they could assess my skills. Unfortunately, I was told that I was a better teacher than the director of the program, and they were concerned that would create difficulties with her.

I did meet with an evaluator from Florida who was qualified to evaluate my skills. She told me how impressed she was in the demonstration class I taught, but also affirmed I was beyond the skill level that would mesh well with their staff.

Next, I applied for a job at Renewal House, a drug abuse treatment program, and was hired as the clinical director based on the wide range of experience I'd gotten while working with drug addicts in California. I began immediately.

With a minimal amount of investigation, I discovered that there were staff clinicians who were both selling drugs to the clients and having sexual relations with them. I called an all-day meeting of the staff three days before I was due to move into my clinical director position, and at the door I left a stack of resignation slips. I started the meeting by reciting all the unethical things I had discovered. I gave them an ultimatum. "If you do not leave this meeting with a plan to clean this up, I will have your resignation slip today."

The first two hours of the session were comprised of bitching and moaning about how unfair all of this was, until one of the participants said, "You know, we're not making a plan here."

By the end of the day, everyone had bought into a plan that would help resolve the problems we had uncovered. The former executive director of Renewal House, who was part of the transition team, came to me with a request that she be compensated for all of her volunteer hours. I recited all of the potential crimes that she was committing with clients in the program, and I asserted that she absolutely did not deserve any compensation for volunteer hours.

On the third day I was there, the legal director came to my office and told me that I was fired. His most sterling criticism of me was that I reminded him of his mother. Nevertheless, I and my integrity were out on the street with no job just three days before Christmas.

Being desperate and needing help on the spot, I called Dr. John Basmajian, known as the godfather of therapeutic biofeedback, at Emory University Research Center. He was the first person who successfully trained a single neuron to fire. He had written a book called Muscles Alive. We had met at a conference involving brainwave biofeedback. He had a wicked sense of humor, and we got along famously. We grokked each other. I knew I could count on him. I told him of my current dire straits.

In the background as I talked with him, I could hear their annual Christmas party going on. John told me to come over immediately, so I went to Emory University to meet with him. He excused himself from the room for a minute and brought back one of the directors for a grant from the National Cancer Institute.

He introduced me to Dr. Carmella Gonnella and told her to hire me on his name. I left his office immediately to prepare for the new on-the-road job. I felt very comfortable traveling around the southeast, interviewing physicians regarding their attitudes toward post-cancer rehabilitation.

John and I continued to enjoy our wonderful and humorous bond. I organized my fellow researchers to contribute to a project, and on his birthday, we presented him with a book called Muscles Between Your Ears, which he treasured—a spoof on his book Muscles Alive—which he treasured. The job lasted for a year, and as a new US president came into office, the National Cancer Institute changed the criteria of the grant and ended my tenure at Emory University.

At the urging of my friend Dale, a local designer, I went to the bank for a startup loan. These were the days when you could walk into a bank and say, "Hi, I'm a doctor," and they would give you $25,000—no collateral, not even a background check! That's when I started my own psychology practice.

I used the money the bank gave me to design and furnish my office in style. It was situated on the top floor of a building called Tower Place that looked like an old camera flash cube—As you walked through the entrance to my office on the top floor, the walls were all covered in grass cloth. It had sparkling glass windows on two sides of the building and the floors were adorned with purple shag rugs. From my therapy office you could look straight down through all twenty-nine floors.

Standing in my office would give you the feeling that you were on the bridge of a spaceship. The massive windows were twelve feet high and forty feet long overlooking all of west Atlanta. I had a large, round glass table with eye-catching metal framework where I would hold my therapy meetings. Much fun of all kinds was had in there, professional and otherwise.

One of the main services I offered to clients was called Video Feedback Therapy. I would position my clients where they would be looking directly into a video camera behind which I sat. After describing to them what negative self-talk sounded like, I would ask them to give me examples of their own negative self-talk. I asked them to imagine that their "negative manager"—the author of their negative thoughts—was in another room watching a TV screen that was hooked up to my camera. I would then ask them to speak directly to that negative manager and say, "Manager, these are the negative things you tell me about myself."

Often, the phrases would be "I'm too fat" or "I'm not smart enough." Other common phrases were "being powerful is dangerous" or "I have no talent." And often, "no one would be attracted to me." The list of negative phrases could go on and on.

Most of these ideas originated in childhood and were deeply implanted in their minds. After they finished vocalizing the negative thoughts to the camera, I would turn to them and ask them several questions: "How does it make you feel when you hear these statements?" "What does it do to your motivation?" "How does it affect your sense of confidence?" Usually, they would report frustration and demotivation as key outcomes of listening to their negative thoughts.

Next, I would ask them to role-reverse and become the negative manager, talking into the camera to themselves. I would then interview the negative manager, asking questions like: "Why do you say these things to Bill?" "What's your purpose?"

Oftentimes, the negative manager believes itself to be helping the person, but—upon interviewing the client—I make sure to point out that helping is the exact opposite of what is actually happening. Next, I would ask the negative manager another round of questions such as, "Whose voice in Bill's childhood do you sound most like?" More often than not the voice is that of an angry or blaming mother or father.

I would say to the negative manager, "You think you are being helpful, but you are not. Rather than helping, you are getting your energy from Bill's abusive parent and using that toxic energy against him. You criticize him, which deflates him just as it used to when his parents did it." After drawing attention to this reality, I would then ask my client if they really want to keep listening to the negative manager. Ninety-nine percent of the time, the answer was a resounding "no."

After the client confronted their negative manager, I would then ask if they would like to listen to a different voice—one that would be supportive and helpful. Of course, they would say "yes." I would say to them, "Now, this time imagine that as you are looking in the camera, you are talking to the voice of Spirit. This is a voice that is calm and clear, connected, creative, and compassionate."

I would ask them to look into the camera, speaking directly to Spirit and say, "I've been very out of touch with you. I've been listening to the voice of the manager, and it's killing me. I want a new voice to listen to—one that's supportive and caring.

I want to listen to you." Then, I would ask them to role-reverse again and become the voice of Spirit. As they looked into the camera at themselves, I would have them repeat after me: "I love you, and I will never leave you. You are precious to me. Nothing you have ever said or done has ever harmed who you really are and you are precious to me."

This is essential in working with people who have been abused in childhood and who have taken unreasonable blame on themselves. Whatever happened to you never harmed who you really are. I would then have them role-reverse again and speak to Spirit.

"Spirit, I'm committed to listening to you. When I hear the voice of the negative manager, I will let it be a reminder to listen to you instead." This is a critical piece because it creates a double bind for the negative manager. If every time it speaks up it becomes a reminder to listen to Spirit, then its voice must become quieter. When I would play the video back to the participant, I'd find a good, forward-facing still frame. Then, I would hold up a square, mirrored tile perpendicular to the screen down the middle of their face. This created a split-screen image. This image allowed them to see what their face would look like if it were either all right-sided or all left-sided.

The left side of the face is connected to the right side of the brain, which is more intuitive and emotional. The double-left side would look warmer, kinder, more compassionate. The right side of the face is connected to the left side of the brain, which is more analytical and is also the home of the critical negative manager. The double right-side face would look colder, more thoughtful, more analytical, often judgmental.

Through this process, the impact on the participant of seeing what he is doing to himself is enormous, and this method was very successful in helping my clients.

As of this writing, my current work with Internal Family Systems, so many decades later, continues to use this video self-talk approach.

I formed a company to offer this video process to a wider market and was using it in management training. Specifically, it was a medical public relations firm by the name of Weiss, Webber, and Halpern. I was Weiss, of course, and Webber was Lana Webber who was an advertising specialist. The Halpern of the group—we will call her Lorna—was a lovely lady who was a lover and a friend.

The firm worked with hospitals and assisted them in making their public relations programs more effective.

My other trajectory was called "InnerView." It was a company focusing on doing sales and executive training. I had built InnerView with a guy named Jim Georges. We would travel around the country to places like Baltimore and New York and do work with major companies such as Coca-Cola and Savin Corporation.

This was all going pretty well for me until my psoriatic arthritis degenerated the bones in my hands to the point where the knuckles had to be surgically replaced. My melting bony knuckles were replaced with plastic ones.

It was around that time—close to the time of the surgery—that I began experiencing severe depression and emotional collapse, and ultimately ended up pulling out of Weiss, Webber, and Halpern and the partnership with Jim Georges.

While I was in the hospital a psychiatrist visited me and administered a cortisol challenge test. This was a test that measured how well a person recovers from stress. The result was that I was not able to produce the hormones and chemicals that kept me afloat. It was very difficult to explain to the members of my company the impact of the depression on my ability to perform. I imploded, falling into a dark place in my life.

The doctor saw the urgency of getting me on an antidepressant and he did. Still my experience of depression was the next major event in my life that challenged my entire worldview. I moved from being sunny and focused to utter dismay and inertia. It was like stepping casually into the Grand Canyon.

My recovery was gradual. The antidepressants began to take hold. As a result, my mood improved and my ability to focus slowly returned.

Around that time, I had met the director of the Johnson O'Connor Research Foundation, which provided testing for children to assist parents in locating appropriate school placement for their child. They worked with adults to find schools that fit their needs as well.

I was looking for a psychological testing package to combine with my InnerView video program. The director wanted me to take her nine-hour battery of aptitude tests which she used with the adults to demonstrate to me the kind of information her tests could produce. After analyzing the results, she peered over her glasses at me and said these fateful words: "In one category, you rank at the one hundred percent level, suggesting you would be an excellent psychologist. And in another, you rank at the one hundred percent level suggesting you would be an excellent musician. If you have a talent and you don't use it, it will bite you in the ass."

A SONG

My senses fill me with god
or, (if you will)
a raindrop in my hand;
tears rushing from my heart
I struggle to grasp that (which
is always greater than)
beautiful thing inside
all men (a song?)

Three weeks after my encounter with the aptitude tester, I took Gina to a jazz club in Atlanta for New Year's Eve. The place was empty except for the pianist, Duke Pearson. He was a world-famous jazz pianist, and I approached him and asked if I could sit in. When he handed me the microphone, I started scat singing. We had a great evening and I was hooked. Soon, I would be singing three nights a week with comedian and jazz pianist Jerry Farber.

The daily schedule for Gina and me had been for me to go to work in my therapy private practice and Gina to go to Georgia Tech as a student. Despite the fact that we had hired tutors to help her, her grades were abysmal. Perhaps, this was related to the fact that she actually didn't go to school and spent most of her time wandering around the upscale Nieman Marcus department store instead. This was a shock to my system and put a damper on my trust level and on our relationship.

I had traveled to Birmingham to conduct a workshop, and once again, my hormones were heightened and got ahold of me as they have off and on throughout my life. They didn't have the term "sexual addiction" back then, or at least I didn't, but my behavior was probably in that arena.

In Birmingham, I met a delightful young lady and, let's say, stayed late. When I got home afterwards, I talked with my friend Bob Bailey and shared with him what had happened. At that point, I'm sure I was in the clutches of a midlife crisis, and when Gina called Bob to ask what was going on, he told her. It was the end of our relationship.

Creampuff

At some point while I was living in Atlanta, I met this woman. I can't recall her name, but she was a major creampuff — with a cherry on top — so we'll just call her Creampuff. She was blonde, and smart, and funny. And married. She was separated from her husband, Richard, and living in her own house.

Creampuff invited me to her house for the evening. As we started undressing, she told me that there was a very slim chance that her estranged husband might show up, and that if he did, I should pick up all of my clothing and shoes and step out the back door onto the back deck and then get dressed. And then get away.

We were lying in bed after making love and falling asleep in each other's arms. Suddenly, I could hear fists beating on the front door. She said, "Oh my God! It's Richard!"

As per her instructions, I picked up all of my clothes and stepped out the back door onto the deck. As I did, a flashlight turned on me at the back of the house and a voice yelled out, "Freeze!"

You know how certain moments of your life seem longer than you would imagine? At that moment, I decided that I was not going to die—naked—on somebody's deck. I backed through the door into the bedroom and started getting dressed.

Meanwhile, Creampuff had gone into the living room and opened the door. She came back to tell me that these men were policemen who were looking for Richard because he had a truckload of unpaid traffic tickets. When they saw my car, they thought I was him. Creampuff went out and explained to them that I was not Richard. She then came back in and said, "They want to see your license."

This was quite awkward as I was only half-dressed—more importantly, half-naked—but I found my license and gave it to her. She showed it to the police, and they left. This event, as funny as it seems now, put a damper on our relationship.

Later, at the end of my relationship with Creampuff, my first wife, Cheryl, came to visit me in Atlanta. I was living in a duplex in a nice section of town, and on the same night that she was there to visit—staying over in a separate bed—the doorbell rang.

It was Creampuff. I felt torn and made the decision to not bring her upstairs because of my concerns about how it might make Cheryl feel. Somehow, I still managed to successfully get my needs met right there on the front lawn. It seems insane now, but at the time it made perfect sense.

The next day, Cheryl told me that she wouldn't have minded if Creampuff had come in, but it was too late for that now. At the time, it was clear which head I was thinking with.

I operated out of a concept of My Invisible Lover. Every relationship with a new woman started off with a big bang, which tended to fizzle into a gray dullness. None of them manifesting the ideal of My Invisible Lover. But Lord knows I kept trying!

ANGELS ON EARTH

Form and all its minions of frightened logic
  Dissolve in a pool of moonlight
   A breathy whisper, a loving touch
Yesterdays of pain, of burrowing in

Are forgotten; wrapped in Irish lace
  Wounds heal and flowers beyond Imagination,
clear as fireworks
     Bloom in your eyes

The sacred other /
   The sacred / the sacred other
     Is invoked; an ancient connection
Restored: "We have always known each Other /

sacred other / sacred other"
Today, we breathe each other into Existence
"Oh lordy, we gonna have a good time"
    We are an invitation to dance
  We are the dance

Hagalamanj: Hold the Light High

I was attending a week-long conference in the Blue Ridge Mountains in North Carolina sponsored by the Sufis—a sect of Islam devoted to peace and the attainment of enlightenment through music, dance, and contemplation. The conference was entitled "Toward a Global Society." People from all over the world were attending, sharing ideas, dancing, and living playfully.

The main speaker was a philosopher named David Spangler, who was the co-director of the Findhorn Community in Scotland, and still a prolific writer. He spoke about the varieties of mythology that we all lived in, the bubble we created around ourselves and out into the world. Each bubble contained beliefs, values, and a distinctive signature that each of us brings to life.

He began to talk about what he called "personal myth." It was represented by the deeply imbedded beliefs we held about our own value, our direction and purpose in life, and an internal guidance system we possessed but were not always aware of.

This was a new idea for me. Not one being imposed on me, but rather a recognition of something I already knew. As he talked, I experienced the audience of 500 people settling into a profound reverie. I realized I was only one of many experiencing this deeper remembrance of self. I always knew that I had a purpose even when I couldn't enunciate its form.

In the center of this conference in the mountains there was another prescheduled event that would be taking place. There was to be an international conference call with members of the Gallucci Family. The Galluccis were an international group of bright thinkers devoted to bringing peace to our planet through fun. If you were a member, you took on that last name, at least with the other members.

The existence of the Galluccis had only been brought to my attention a few months earlier by Fred Lehrman, a trainer for Loving Relationships Training, who also happened to be at the same conference this day. Fred had told me to get in contact with Marc Sarkady, the originator of the Gallucci Family and also a well-known consultant on both business and international political projects.

The first step he had taken in creating the Gallucci Family was to name himself Marco Gallucci. I had been immediately struck by the consonance with both my sense of humor and the sincerity of my desire for peace and on being given his contact information had immediately reached out to him about joining the family.

Toward the end of the first day of the conference, I stood up and made an announcement to the attendees. I said that I had a speakerphone in my room and was going to participate in a worldwide conference call sponsored by the Gallucci Family. In this call, the Family would enact a marriage ceremony for everyone in the world. To my surprise, twenty people stood up, stating that they were Galluccis and would bring snacks.

We all packed into my hotel room and at exactly eight o'clock we called in to the network of Galluccis. Our first step was to have each group from the city or country state their names and locations and, briefly, describe what they were doing to promote world peace. We spoke about the different projects we were working on while sharing an extraordinary feeling of camaraderie.

People were on the call from Moscow; Paris; Barangay, New Zealand; New York City; and Los Angeles, and each spoke briefly. We were then paired with some other locations in the world and for five minutes shared more in-depth information about our activities, which were all aligned with the goals of the family.

Our group was connected to a group in Barangay, New Zealand. It was exciting to be joined in this novel and powerful way. At one point, Paul Winter of the Paul Winter Consort—and also another Gallucci—played a flute solo, and a Russian woman from Moscow read a poem. We were then witness to a wedding between the East Coast Galluccis, represented by Marc Sarkady, and the West Coast Galluccis, represented by Marilyn Ferguson— author of the popular book The Aquarian Conspiracy.

The closing ceremony created a sense of oneness. When it was over, we became quiet, absorbing feelings and connections that would stay with us for life.

Upon returning to Atlanta after the conference, I continued my involvement in the Gallucci Family. In order to officially become a Gallucci, we were required to take on a Gallucci name, so I became Cuneo Gallucci. The Galluccis had also developed their own language, which I was also attempting to master.

I engaged in another worldwide Gallucci event, entitled "World War IV." The premise of WW IV was that, should WWIII take place, it would mean the total annihilation of all life on planet earth, so we decided to skip over it and make WWIV a war of LOVE. This truly felt like a family event. I purchased a khaki army shirt and had a heart patch on my sleeve, the name Cuneo on the chest, and the Gallucci Family on the back, and I proudly represented the family and everything we stood for.

There was something immensely confirming about being a Gallucci. I realized early in the game that this family was full of extremely bright and committed people, willing to open themselves and risk being ridiculed, if only to touch one person's mind, to let one person know that they're not alone.

MY FORCES ARE GATHERING

I meet very few people who can imagine
  Someone like me
Those exalted imaginers who can
    Are strung across the world
    Like way stations
We send each other strong messages
   "I remember you with pleasure
     And remind you to pay attention."
To stay aware

2 tbsps.	Be bright
1-1/4 cups	Stay in touch
3 oz. (grated)	Call out your love
40 lbs. well mixed	Be generous

Continue mixing
  I dream of money enough
  To have a network convention
   In Tahiti
I am condensing now
  Putting it together
   Putting me together

I am condensing now
You remember me with pleasure
And remind me to pay attention
And I love you in return

⁓⃝⁓

Later, when I would move up to Memphis, Tennessee, the activities of the Gallucci family would be declining, but I have always felt—and still do feel—connected to Marco Gallucci.

Years later, I would have the chance to reconnect with Marc Sarkady over lunch. We sat together and reminisced, laughed, and fell silent. In the depth of that connection, Marco Gallucci began to cry, and I joined him. These were what I call sacred tears.

I would see Marco one more time, some years later. We talked about the possibility of resurrecting the Gallucci Family. Nothing much came of it. It went its way as is true of many peak experiences. It embeds itself in our psyche and in our hearts. We are enriched, watered from a sacred fountain, and then off to the rest of life. For me, the Galluccis polished another facet of the gem of my weird and quirky life story and provided me with a heart-connection with people around the world seeking peace.

My Last Acid Trip
on the Island of Kona in Hawaii, 1983

I remember bare feet, bare body on a black cliff. Standing; the raw power Naked on the edge of a cliff on Kona, Hawaii; energy shooting up my LSD-infused spine in the slow lurching explosion of Pacific water shooting sixty feet into a funnel toward a languid, summer landscape. Black sand, a perfect frame for the ocean's blue-green inexhaustible theater. A wry quiet voice spoke through me into the sparkling blue immensity. After a long pause, I heard a voice in my head saying, "Well, that's it." That was the end of my psychedelic journeying.

Maxx Schnallinger

I had been struggling with a bout of depression, and as a result, my practice in Atlanta had diminished by 1984. In spite of the circumstances I was facing, I had been working with a fascinating guy named Maxx Schnallinger. Maxx, who was born in Austria, was a massive and beautiful man. He had a towering stature, at about six-foot-four, and had the most strange and wonderful Germanic accent. He was very bright. I had been working with Maxx and his wife Dorothy in Parent Effectiveness Training to help their rebellious son, and over the course of time, Maxx had really taken a liking to me. We decided to do some work together.

Maxx and I went from Atlanta to Chicago as consultants in order to evaluate some of the top Chicago restaurants. We had plans for several additional projects together. When we got to Chicago, I promised him that I would take him to a jazz club so he could hear me sing. After we had investigated two or three top-flight restaurants we headed back to the hotel and asked the concierge where we might find a good jazz club.

He recommended a club called Milt's, which was owned by a singing and performing group, the Trenier Brothers. Here was Milt Trenier, one of the original brothers, who often performed on the Ed Sullivan show as a Las Vegas-type act. It was getting late, but we went to the club, and it was almost empty of people. I went up to Milt and told him I was a scat singer and told him a little bit about who I had sung with, and he agreed to let me sit in.

It was the last set, and Maxx and I were sitting at the bar. As the set started to close, I realized that Milt was not about to let me sing with him. I went up to him as the band was closing down and asked him why he didn't call me up to sing. He looked at me, somewhat disparagingly, and said, "Do you think you could've cut it with a band like this?" I told him I could have blown him off the stage.

Since the band was breaking down their instruments, Maxx and I left the club and caught a cab. I was disappointed that I had promised Maxx that he could hear me sing, and as we were driving away in the cab, I looked into the front seat and saw a tenor saxophone. I asked the cab driver if he was a musician and he said that he was. He said that he carried his tenor saxophone with him wherever he drove in the taxi so that he could practice during his down time. When we pulled up in front of our hotel, I said, "Let's play," so he got out his saxophone, and for a half hour, he and I gave Maxx a private jazz concert. Maxx was thrilled, and I felt like I had fulfilled my promise.

On a spiritual note, I had also become very involved with Loving Relationships Training. I had a good friend, Steve Roffwarg, who I attended a weekend workshop with for rebirthing. The workshop was designed by spiritual leader Sondra Ray. One Sunday, when Sondra Ray stood up front with Helen Schucman's book A Course in Miracles, I felt what I like to call "God shivers." One week later, the editor for A Course in Miracles, Ken Wapnick, was speaking in Atlanta. I heard him speak extensively on the Course, and it was life-changing.

Clark Terry

Clark Terry is one of the greatest jazz trumpet players in the world and probably the most famous scat singer. He had played with Count Basie and was featured with the band on the Johnny Carson Show. He was world-renowned. I was living in Atlanta when I first met him.

∽🙞🙜∾

BRIGHT MOMENT: I was in St. Louis for a conference and took a walk in the hotel neighborhood. Right next door to the hotel I saw that he was playing with his band. I was thrilled. I walked into the middle of an energetic music session. I sat and watched in amazement at my good luck. During the break, I asked him if I could sit in with him. He very generously opened a spot for me, and we did two or three tunes, to our mutual delight.

∽🙞🙜∾

ANOTHER BRIGHT MOMENT: I ran into him again when I was conducting a training workshop in Buffalo, New York. Clark was performing with a big band in an extraordinary concert hall that was shaped like an egg. After the concert, my friend and I went backstage. Clark embraced me and said that he wished he had known I was coming—he would have invited me to sing with him. We parted ways in the hallway, each going in opposite directions, not realizing that the hallway was circular. We met again at the elevator. Clark was accompanied by a student who was urging him to get back to the hotel because he had to get up early in the morning to catch a plane.

The moment that the elevator doors closed on us, I began scat-singing a bass line, and he immediately began scat-singing a melody on top of it. We kept on trading choruses. We were entranced, and when the elevator doors opened, we didn't want to leave. Finally, after a few more choruses and some insistence on the part of the student, we left one another. Here's the kicker: the next day, I sent him a letter claiming that our collaboration was the best elevator music I had ever heard.

∽᷼ᴽᴽᵒᐧᴄᐧ᷼

Clark had been planning on getting married in Dallas, Texas, and he invited me to come to the wedding. Two months later, I was on a plane to attend the festivities. Clark had suffered a stroke sometime before the wedding, shortly after the first time I had met him, and he was recovering. I got a chance to sing with saxophonist Red Holloway, bassist Milt Hinton, and trombonist Al Foster at the wedding. Clark's daughter, an excellent jazz violinist, performed as well. It was a fabulous night.

The Lark and the Dove

Aside from having the best Caesar salad in Atlanta, The Lark and the Dove also featured Jerry Farber, a well-known comedian and jazz pianist. As I mentioned, I sang with Jerry two or three nights a week for many years. Richard, the barback for the restaurant, took a powerful dislike toward my scat singing and complained to the owner that they should get rid of me. Jerry put his job on the line and said, "If he goes, I go." This act of defiance endears him to me to this day.

MEMPHIS

Wes, the Dog Bite, and Moving to Memphis

Maxx Schnallinger and his wife were design consultants to a guy in Memphis, Tennessee—we'll call him "Wes"— for a massive remodel of a world-famous hotel. They had accomplished the initial revamping of the inside of the hotel and then went on to design several other attractions housed within the structure. Wes was the general manager and had been at odds with others who were involved in the renovation project, so Maxx convinced him that he should start coming down to Atlanta a few days a week to consult with me regarding management of the hotel.

While he was down there, I began helping Wes to organize an executive committee that would ultimately serve as a buffer between the others involved in the project and himself. Finally, after several visits with me in Atlanta, Wes implored me to move to Memphis. He followed this by promising, "I will pay you $50,000 a year. You can set up your own practice, and you can help me set up my executive committee."

I was burned out on Atlanta anyway, so at this point, I thought to myself, I'm going to do this. I had packed up all of my things and was literally sitting on my boxes when I called and reminded him, "Wes, I still don't have a signed contract."

"Oh. Yeah. Well, see, there's kind of a problem with that," he stammered. "I can't really give you $50,000—I can only give you $25,000."

By the time he told me that, I had already closed my practice down and was living in a room filled with nothing but boxes. As I looked around, I said to myself, Fuck it. I'm just going to go.

It was October 1984 when I made the move to Memphis. As soon as I got there, I rented a house and began working with some clients.

I was also still working with Wes, advising him regarding the executive committee. He had been having problems with one human resources guy in particular and when I expressed my opinion about the situation to Wes, he ended up firing me on the spot. It was sudden, and as I found out later, not uncharacteristic of him.

As if that wasn't bad enough, to add insult to injury, my abrupt dismissal was immediately followed by his dog biting me. His dog was a standard poodle—tall and stately with large, dark, oval-shaped eyes. To this day, I cannot erase the memory of the thought that flew through my mind when it happened. When that dog bit me, I had a vision. An image flashed before my eyes in which I was picking up a phone and smashing it into that poodle's head and smearing his brain onto the walls.

Wes's family had an abundance of lawyers, so expending too much energy into a lengthy legal battle with him would be futile. We ended up settling for a mere $7.000—a far cry from the $50,000 that had been promised to me before moving to Memphis.

After the dog bite incident and having the murderous vision I'd had, I was horrified, so I went home and called Jack Donahue, a friend that I had met at a conference on rebirthing in

Hilton Head, South Carolina. Right from the moment we met, Jack and I became good friends. I told him about the incident that had occurred with the dog and confessed to him the disturbing and gory visualization I had when it happened. Jack responded by asking how long I thought it would take for me to forgive myself for the violent thoughts I had towards the poodle that day.

I told him, "Probably a year." He said, "Are you certain that you will be able to let this go in a year?" I confidently said, "In a year." In all of his infinite wisdom, he countered by asking me, "If you are certain that you can do it in a year, then why not do it now?" He short-circuited the forgiveness process for me.

Big Dog Parties

When I arrived in Memphis, I sought out every New Age and spiritual teacher I could find, and within two months, I had begun throwing parties at my house which we called "Big Dog" parties. The title was derived from an expression in the black community that was "party like a big dog." To me, this meant that when a big dog goes out to play, he doesn't care what other people think. He is not afraid.

Within two more months, over a hundred people would attend these parties every time. I entitled the parties "Intergalactic Potluck Parties," which meant that you could bring food from any planet. This included Mars Bars, Moon Pies, etc. Almost all of the food was vegetarian, extremely tasty, and supplied me with a week's worth of food after the party. I supplied plasticware, plates, sodas, bottled water, and ice. The house I lived in was perfect for these parties. It had a huge space where we could roll the rug back and dance.

People would say to me, "I love your parties because I get to be with all the people I love but never get to see." The way I set it up requested every party participant to put on a nametag that included their first name and their spiritual name.

The person's spiritual name was derived from the quality they most wanted to develop in their own life, followed by the suffix "ananda," which means "bliss" in Sanskrit. For example, my spiritual name was "Hugananda," in other words, he who gains bliss from hugging. My friend Earl chose "Peaceananda," and my friend Anne chose "Healananda".

Another facet of the parties was that I would place a five-foot-wide helium balloon on my front lawn and ask people to write their highest thoughts for the planet in permanent markers on blank labels and stick them onto the balloon. Toward the end of the party, everyone would gather on the front lawn and release the five-foot balloon, sending our highest thoughts into the stratosphere.

In the year or two during which we had these monthly big dog parties, only one person got drunk enough to be sent home in a cab.

Seeking Spirituality

In Memphis I sought out the spiritual leaders in the community. The foremost leader was Earl Purdy, a Course in Miracles teacher, numerologist, astrologer, and my African American brother from another mother. I had already become familiar with the Course and began to co-lead five Course in Miracles classes a week with Earl, and we also hung out all the time. Boy, did we have some adventures!

Our interactions influenced the way I did therapy. I had a number of different projects I was working on that were all influenced by him. One of his greatest values for me was to keep me focused on simply reading the Course in Miracles, without the requirement that I understand it or believe it or even accept it. In that sense, he was a kind of a fundamentalist—his message was: Just read the Course. Just read the Course and see what happens.

WHEN I'M CHANGIN'

When I'm changin'
I'm changing the world

Every time I choose
For Peace
    Life
        God
My eyes clear up

I see the happy dream
Bright beyond my eyes
Songs beyond my ears

Every time I choose for Ego
    Fear
        Death
My eyes go dark
I see the nightmare

I have taught it consistently every Sunday for thirty-five years now. It has been a real core of my spirituality and philosophy in my life.

Another thing happened around the time arrived in Memphis. One of the ministers of a church called Connections Church, which was a New Age center, said that she had been praying for someone to come and teach a breathing technique called rebirthing—and then I showed up. Rebirthing had been part of Loving Relationships Training in which I had previously gotten certified.

In this breathing technique you do what is called "connected breathing," where you breathe very, very powerfully up into the chest, and go as high as you can, and then immediately release into the exhale, and then immediately pull up again. You are breathing in to your power, out into pleasure.

Often when people practice this, they have profound experiences that take them all the way back into a birth process, or into childhood which can release them from some traumatic experience they've faced in the past. For a year, I taught a free class on rebirthing upstairs in my house, and I later integrated the exercise into my practice.

Dying for the Second Time: *Death by Pigeon Poop*

In 1986, I was just completing a thirty-day training program in New York to become a center manager for Loving Relationships Training. Toward the end of the training, I began to have fever and chills. I went to see a doctor in New York who immediately hospitalized me, and—miracle of all miracles—he was able to conduct three different tests while I was in the hospital. He said to me, "Whatever this is, it's complex. I hate complex things. I think you should go back to Memphis where you have a support group and find out what this is."

So, I scheduled a flight for Saturday afternoon.

As soon as I got back to Memphis, I contacted all my friends and my personal physician Dan Marshall. I set up an appointment to meet with Dan on Monday. In the meantime, I went out to Blues Alley to sing with the band. On Monday, Dan recognized the seriousness of my symptoms and drove me to the emergency room at Methodist Hospital. He stayed with me for five hours until he could get me into a room.

Within a day, every diagnostician in town was on my case. Some doctors believed I had AIDS while others sought more mundane solutions. By Wednesday, I was bleeding out of every orifice. I remember a young medical resident named Jim Andrews helping me to get to the bathroom. Jim's grip on my arm startled me. I had no idea I was so weak. Naked under my hospital gown, I was in the hands of a twenty-five-year-old who was doing his best to hide his fear. The cold commode, wet with my blood, caused me to focus suddenly. I looked into his eyes and asked, "Is this it?"

He knew immediately the meaning of my question. Instinctively, he connected with my eyes and said, "You are not going to die."

I knew he was lying, trying to mask his uncertainty. He knew that I was going down rapidly. Ten doctors were feverishly trying to figure out why my immune system had collapsed. I was shivering and burning up at the same time. The next thing I knew, I was suddenly on a gurney, being pushed through long-hanging sheets of semi-transparent plastic. The light of life went out in my eyes. I was dead, but on life support. For the next thirty days I would experience many drug-induced hallucinations.

By Thursday, my parents had flown in from California, basically to attend my funeral. My dear friend Diane had flown up the night before to look after me. My mother later reported to me their surprise when they walked into my hospital room to find Diane circling my bed reciting a Hindu chant, "Om namashi vayu. Om namashi vayu." Diane looked up at my parents and said, "He likes this."

By now, a diagnosis had been reached. Apparently, I had taken too high of a dose of methotrexate (an immunosuppressant), and it had successfully suppressed my immune system so that—standing on the fire escape at Bonnie and David's apartment, where I was staying in New York—I had contracted histoplasmosis from the pigeon poop which covered the banisters on their balcony. We had been watching the Macy's Thanksgiving Day Parade processing right in front of the apartment.

Waking up from my coma seemed easy enough. I opened my eyes and found I was in a well-lit medical intensive unit with people who defined the word "bustling." Apparently, Dr. Tower's plan to keep me breathing until my immune system kicked back in was paying off. I was face down and trying to talk out of the side of my mouth.

A nurse noticed my efforts and called Dr. Tower to my side. He leaned close and my first words to him were . . .

"Two old Jewish men meet on the beach in Miami."

Sam says to Max, "Nu? Max, I haven't seen you in many months. Vhere have you been?"

Max replies, "I vent out vest" (translate to west for the goyim and then translate goyim as gentiles).

"Vhat were you doing out vest?" asks Sam.

"I vas a cowboy," says Max.

"Vhat?" says Sam. "You're seventy-four years old. Vhat vere you doing?"

"I vas ridin' and ropin' and punchin' cattle."

'So vhat happened?'

"Vell," says Max, "one day, we're ridin' along, and over a hill comes hundreds of Indians chasing us vith guns and bows and arrows, hoopin' and hollerin', and ve're riding as fast as ve can.

"So ve take a left toin (turn). Big mistake. It's a box canyon, and ve're trapped. Ve run out of ammunition, and dey don't."

Sam is incredulous. "So vhat happened?"

"I died." says Max.

"Vhat?" says Sam. "How could this be? You're standing right here. You're living!"

"Oi!" says Max. "You call this living?"

Dr. Tower got angry at me for being frivolous. He clearly did not understand my sense of humor.

The absence of the methotrexate allowed my immune system to reboot and I recovered.

So, about those hallucinations. In my mind I was in a glass enclosed room overhanging Beale Street in Memphis. On the outer edges of the room were giant purple toadstools for chairs. I fell in love with a wonderful nurse who never suspected my undying love. It wasn't the first nurse I fell in love with over time.

Beth

A while back I had become connected with a group of New Age people that all met at a health food store called Honey Suckle. Every Saturday they would serve genuine Indian food, and we would come to eat and schmooze. Behind the counter was Beth, the woman who would soon become my third wife (but who's counting?). She was a singer with The Memphis Horns and also a student of A Course in Miracles. She had a beautiful three-year-old boy named Jamel.

Beth and I were attracted to each other and quickly formed a relationship. Within a month, we were in a committed relationship. Within four months, we were married.

I had made a decision in my mid-twenties that I would not father a child due to my fears that I would pass on the painful consequences of my psoriatic arthritis, so having Jamel in my life brought me great joy. I had a mutually supportive relationship with Beth's ex-husband, James, an incredibly talented musician.

Bobby McFerrin

The smell of the Orpheum Theatre in Memphis was unmistakable—old chairs and ancient furnishings. Two thousand people were anxiously awaiting Bobby McFerrin, the international "Don't Worry, Be Happy" singer. Beth had picked me up a half an hour before the concert as I had flown in from a consulting job in Tucson. We were rushing to make it to the concert on time. We made it.

I had chosen these seats, tenth row, center aisle, because I knew he would jump off the stage into the audience. I was absolutely certain of this.

From backstage, I could hear the whistling theme of "Don't Worry, Be Happy," and this small and relaxed black man stepped onto the stage and everything became electric. Half the audience was whistling along with him. I was exactly where I wanted to be without knowing why.

⚮

BRIGHT MOMENT: After the third song, Bobby jumped off the stage and walked up the center aisle. I had total certainty that he was going to come to me. He was talking to the audience and walked right past me. After he bypassed me, he went about three rows beyond me and stopped. He turned and came back to stand next to me.

"Hi!" he said, "What's your name?"
"Mark Weiss," flows out of me.
He asked me, "Has anyone ever written a song about your name?"
"No, they haven't."

He started singing using a 5/4 rhythm, a la "Take Five" by Dave Brubeck, "Mark Weiss, Mark Weiss, Mark Weiss, Mark Weiss." He was singing in this lopsided rhythm. Spontaneously, I began to sing a blues bass line in a loud, booming bass voice. He stopped, surprised and delighted, and began to scat sing on top of my bass line.

After a few choruses, he started singing a bass line and I started improvising above it. Every cell in my body was vaporized and projecting out of my mouth. The excitement was coursing through every sound. As we closed the set, the audience erupted, screaming and applauding. A peace came over me. I saw his smile and he could see mine. And the concert went on.

In the middle of the concert Mr. McFerrin asked if anyone wanted to come on stage and be part of his background chorus. My wife was so excited that she jumped onto the stage in one leap. I took the stairs. We joined a chorus of fifteen people on stage. He gave us the riffs and he improvised on top of them.

An additional thrilling moment. At the end of the concert, he invited me to audition for a chorus he was putting together called the Voicestra (as in orchestra). I did not pursue this invitation as it would have entailed redirecting my life and not giving me space to develop professionally as a psychologist.

More on Beth

Things had started off great between Beth and me, but after three years of marriage, we decided to get a divorce. We had learned over time that we had different values and we just couldn't see eye to eye, so we decided it was best to go our separate ways.

As we were in the process of our separation, I discovered that Beth had moved in with a man named David. I needed to deliver legal documents to Beth regarding our divorce, but because I was emotionally triggered, I decided that I would drop them off at David's house without calling ahead first. Jamel spotted me coming and went into the house to tell his mother. Beth interpreted my unannounced arrival as stalking her, and that really damaged what was left of our relationship.

We'd made an agreement in mediation that I would pay for her to get her college degree if she would continue to allow me access to Jamel. After she labeled me as a stalker, she told Jamel not to share with me anything personal about his home life at Beth and David's house. This put a huge damper on the communication with my Jamel. In order to continue spending time with him I went through his father James.

When we went to the circus or the movies or just to play video games, as Jamel was sworn to not share the details of his life, there were many times when we rode together in silence over a period of years. I did not want to be part of a small-war-consciousness as I thought that was harmful to him.

I will always remember one particular night when we were riding down Poplar Avenue. We had a conversation discussing how I was no longer his stepfather. I'd asked him what he would say if people asked him who that guy is that's always with him. He said he would tell them I was his friend. I said to him, "If we were friends, and I bought you lunch on a Wednesday, the following Wednesday, you would buy me lunch, but I always buy you lunch." I told him about my godparents in Brooklyn, and we decided that I would be his godfather.

For me it was a spiritual discipline, the most important piece of which was that I never put Jamel in the space of having to violate his mother's rules. In that sense, our relationship became deeper, each of us following Beth's rules, but growing to love each other more just the same. This was some of the most demanding personal work I would ever do.

We stayed close over the years, and later, when Jamel was in college, I would be able to help him work through some emotional issues that were bothering him related to relationships. Now he's in his forties, married with two children of his own, and we still have a great relationship. Over the years I have striven to live in that balance of connection and honor.

My Fiancé, Sherry

Sometime in the late eighties, I met a woman named Sherry through my friend Anne Gillis, a minister of Connections Church in Memphis. Sherry was a student of A Course in Miracles and that was a draw to me.

There didn't seem to be much emotional energy between us at the time. In our second meeting, a month later, there was more of a sense of attraction. We began to date. I took Sherry to meet my mother in Los Angeles. My father had died sometime before. My mother said of her that Sherry was very attractive and had "presence."

She was a real estate agent in Memphis, and I was looking for a house. We had decided to move in together, and discovered a cute house in midtown, a desirable location in Memphis if you could ignore the drug house across the street.

While we were living together, she made very little effort to do her real estate, so I carried the burden financially. That July, I took her with me to Copenhagen to meet my friends and for me to perform. The trip went fine and we returned to business as usual in Memphis once it was over, although Sherry still had not produced any income despite her protests of wanting to be independent.

Over the course of the next year, tensions began to rise and the relationship began to deteriorate. Sherry was still showing no effort to sell houses, and I remember her asking me if, in a relationship, it was okay to lie. Intuitively I knew that if I answered no it wasn't going to stop her from lying, and if I said yes and she seemed relieved, then we had some major trust issues.

She had been going to Native American therapeutic workshops without me, which I discovered later, and as the time for me to go to Copenhagen again in July approached, she had no money to contribute to the trip. Since I didn't have a large budget, I went without her.

When I arrived home, we agreed to meet at a restaurant, and on the way there, I stopped at the house and discovered an American Express bill for $4,000. Sherry had flown to Mexico and attended a spiritually oriented workshop in the Native American tradition, and she had charged all her expenses to my card.

As we sat down for lunch, I showed her the bill and told her of my surprise at this expenditure, since for a year she had been living off of me. The moment I brought it up, she jumped up and ran out of the restaurant.

When we met back at the house, I asked for her to return my engagement ring. With a slight hesitation, she gave it to me, and within a week, she had moved some of her furniture out. She left some of it behind in partial payment for what she owed me. I was beyond angry and took her to court. The court proceedings turned out to be a fiasco in which the judge withheld judgement for six months while it lay on her desk.

AFGE—Another fucking growth experience.

Internal Family Systems

Early in the 2000's I met Dick Schwartz in a conference on Internal Family Systems (IFS) in Nashville. His teachings and book Internal Family Systems completely turned the whole concept of psychotherapy on its head for me.

As I sat in the audience at that Marriage and Family Therapist conference, I was struck that everything Dick said I could check off my list of everything I believed in and had been teaching for half a century. I knew that the most powerful force in a person's life is shaped by their inner conversation with themselves.

Dick clarified that instead of there being a single inner child within us, that each of us is comprised of many different parts, some of whom were formed when we were wounded in trauma events and others formed in success events. Our core is centered in what Dick called "Self." The eight C-word qualities of Self he stated were: Calm, Clear, Compassionate, Creative, Connectedness, Courageous, Curiosity, and Confidence, and what I called Spirit.

I was deeply struck by the resonance I felt both in Dick himself and the Internal Family Systems model which had to do with healing the various parts of us that had been traumatized.

MY DREAMS

My dreams
It always seems
The voices heard are others'

The 'I' that wakes
The sense it makes
Are echoes and their brothers

Only now I've learned to ask
My shadow world of parts
To speak to me
To help me see
The message of their hearts

❦

At the end of the first conference, I went to Dick and asked him to sign my copy of his book and he signed, "I am honored by your enthusiasm." Enthusiasm means "to be filled with the spirit of God."

I was so impressed that I organized a group of therapists in Memphis to go back to Nashville to hear Dick speak again. At the end of the second conference all seven of the therapists came to me and asked if I would be their mentor in IFS. I told them I hadn't even taken the first-level training. They said to me, "Yeah, but you get it." So, I mentored that group for a year at no expense.

Following that second conference, I went to five different levels of training in IFS. Some in Chicago and others in Big Sur in California. I currently have completely integrated the work outlined in his later books No Bad Parts and You are

Greater than the Sum of Your Parts into every aspect of therapy that I do. It is a way I have found that integrates my spiritual path with the rich and powerful energy of body-mind therapy.

Personally, I was able to visualize the core piece of my autoimmune overreaction resulting in my psoriatic arthritis. It looked to me like a speeding cyclone composed of anger and fear related to my father. I managed to invite this cyclone into a safe space. I invited the other therapists in our class to join me in going inside to meet this cyclone.

With the addition of some Emotional Freedom Technique tapping—or EFT (based on EMDR, Eye Movement Desensitization Reprocessing)—to calm my fears, I was able to relax that area of myself and slow the cyclone down. I began to see it as a polarity in which I was afraid of my anger, and my anger was afraid of my fear. The group was very supportive, and over a forty-five-minute session, I was able to stop the cyclone, separate the energies, and for a moment experienced nothing but emptiness.

As one of my therapist friends put it to me, the image that came to his mind was that of a double helix. The moment, he said that I was able to see the double helix in place moving slowly in my gut, I was able to totally surround it with a loving energy of my Higher Self. That image of a slowly rotating double helix, surrounded by loving energy, has stayed with me and gives me great comfort. At this point in my life, I was undoubtedly on the path of healing.

I continue to use IFS in my practice and in my relationships to this day.

Naked Around Bonfires and Learning to Trust.

As a stepping stone to my growth process was my participation in what was then called the "New Warrior Training" (later re-named The Mankind Project). It entailed a weekend in the woods with twenty other men. The experience was designed to help us explore what manhood meant to us through experience rather than words. There we were, twenty men—black and white, old and young, novice and elder—with our backs to the wall talking about what the weekend would be for us.

Many of us had never really talked openly about what it was to be a man, and many of us had a vastly distorted picture of what that means. Some of us thought we knew what it meant to be a man, and some of us and no idea at all. On the faces of every man were wounds—visible wounds—and in the eyes, you could also see a glimmer of hope. Hope that we could discover and unleash new powers surrounding our masculinity that could enrich our lives and restore or allow us to create loving relationships.

As each of us stepped into the lodge on Friday night, we were photographed and shown to a large room where we sat on the floor. I knew some of the men from previous workshops. I was excited to have an opportunity to "stretch"—to reach out and experience the dichotomy of the struggles and the highs, and the balance of these two within my own maleness.

Many of the participants had read a book by Robert Bly called Iron John. Each of us was asked to share our goals for the weekend and issues we felt the New Warrior Training would address. Some of the older men—elders—laid out the structure of the weekend. I had some concerns about my ability to perform various physical tasks because of the arthritis, but I had learned through many other personal growth seminars to trust in the process and ask for help if I needed it. We were shown to our bunks and most of us slept that anticipatory, exciting sleep in which the body is preparing for adventure.

The next morning, we ate a simple breakfast and assisted in the building of the sweat lodge. A sweat lodge is a powerful, transformative tool given to us by Native Americans. Its purpose for them was the same as ours—to create an environment that would lift us beyond our normal consciousness in order to prepare for spiritual awakening.

The one we were building was large enough in size to accommodate twenty men and the outer surface was covered with black plastic. While we were building the sweat lodge, other participants were building a large fire in the center of which were three or four large rocks that had been heated since the wee hours of the morning.

We all took our clothes off and entered the sweat lodge, sitting on the muddy floor in silence. One by one, the large rocks were lifted, balanced on wooden branches and deposited in a large hole in the center of the earthen floor. The leader of the sweat lodge sat by a large pot of water with a ladle in it. As we began, the leader ladled water onto the hot rocks, creating an intense, steaming environment.

Generally, the sweat lodge involves four rounds in which everyone periodically leaves the sweat lodge and stands outside for a while and then re-enters. I really wanted to stay in through all four rounds, and since none of the elders objected, I was allowed to do that. As the fourth round was coming to an end, I had a powerful vision, a kind of remembrance.

Months earlier, I had been watching TV and saw a man with a mustache with a concert tuba in front of him with no mouthpiece. He moved closer to it and started blowing rhythmically into it, a sound that resembled a freight train starting. Once he built up sufficient speed, the camera shifted to four very white people singing "Chattanooga Choo-Choo." The man playing the tuba was my father. As I remembered that in the steaming recesses of the sweat lodge, some inner wisdom came to me and said, "If it weren't for this man's sperm, I wouldn't be sitting in this sweat lodge, much less be alive." This shift in the way I saw my father's contribution to my life opened a door for me and I felt a weight drop from my shoulders.

Shortly after the sweat lodge, all the naked men were taken to a single shower with freezing water coming out, and we had to jump in the shower and brave the intense shock. This was another theme of the New Warrior Training, which was "Don't think about it—just do it." Once we returned to the lodge, still naked, we were taken through an experience in which we were asked to visualize ourselves floating down a river in a boat, getting off the boat and coming to an area in the woods. We were then asked to visualize what animal most represented who we really are, our totem animal. Fairly quickly, the image of a cougar came to my mind. I identified with the aloneness of the cougar, who has a sixty-mile radius of hunting that he governs, for the most part, alone. The leader, who knew something about my musical background, said, "We're going to call you 'Singing Cougar'." I was very happy with that, and I still am.

After the naming ceremony, we all sat together as a group and Ralph, one of the elders, pulled out a bag with three or four different sized dildos. We passed one of the dildos around as if it were a talking stick. Suddenly, out of the group poured myths and fears and laughter and embarrassment as each of us revealed our thoughts about our own penises and our perception of others. One Black man in the group bemoaned the fact that white people assumed that Black men had large penises and his was actually middle-class. We talked about masturbation, failure and success experiences with women, and occasionally men. It was refreshing, energizing, and highly reflective.

Later, we dressed and began some Gestalt experiences in which we acted out relationship issues that had plagued many of us. At one point, I got up and talked about my difficult relationship with my father. The leader of this process asked one man to represent my father and for the rest of the men to form two parallel columns, across which, they joined hands. It was my task to push my way through that column to reach my father. I could feel the rage in my body as I accessed the years of suppressed anger I had felt toward him. I was unable to break through the line, and I immediately fell into a depression.

One of the leaders looked at me and said, "You're choosing death over life."

I could barely speak. The leader had me lie on the floor and threw an old gray blanket over me. I called on every person in my life that had ever been supportive, including my godson, Jamel. Nothing worked. I lay there quietly, and after a while, the leaders left the room, and a kind of banter started up among the participants, making fun of the animal names. The most absurd and hilarious name that came up was "Flying Tapeworm."

I got really mad and, pulling off the gray blanket, I shouted, "You guys are interfering with my depression!" at which everybody laughed. When the leaders came back, I asked to go through that exercise again, and this time, I broke through to my father, but I noticed that I was no longer raging. I hugged the man who was playing my father and experienced gratitude. After the exercise, we ate dinner quietly. Most of the men were introspective. After dinner, we took off our clothes again and ran, naked, through the woods until we came to a huge bonfire.

To the sound of drums, we danced around the fire, yelling into the darkness, touching on primitive places within and feeling a great sense of freedom. We rejoiced in the sense of camaraderie we had earned by being genuine and courageous.

WARRIOR

I am a man without tradition
    without script
    hanging from the Moon God
    by choice, skin of my teeth
    taking jazz from black men
    and love from women
    joy from the children I never was
    God is the author of my invisible play
    and now I jump into warrior water
    immersing myself in synthesis
    of tradition
    breathing safety into my cold bones

❧

The next day, as our experience came to an end, we were photographed, and before-and-after pictures were posted. The contrast was startling. In my second picture, I looked ten years younger and clearly more vital, and the same occurred for almost everyone there.

Life and Death in the Twenty-first Century

In 1994, my best friend and my father both died within five days of one another. I got a chance to practice all the stuff I write about on a very personal level. It started with Jack. My friend. It was hard not to be in awe of Jack. At fifty-nine, he possessed an Irish ferocity about life that was hard to find anywhere. He traveled everywhere and was into everything that fascinated me about life.

When I met Jack eleven years before, he was legally blind from retinitis pigmentosa. His range of sight was very small, and yet he read and walked. He had a powerful charisma and each time I saw him had dropped off more of the pretenses of life and gained more wisdom. His mind was impeccably sharp and our laughter together was uproarious.

Of all Jack's achievements, his highest to me was that he fell in love. He opened his heart and jumped on the sleigh ride we call a relationship, moved to a new house in Massachusetts, determined to remain open till the day he died. I spoke to Jack and his fiancé Andree for an hour and a half on a Wednesday night. Jack had been having heart problems and was in a lot of pain. What I remember from that conversation was that I got Jack to laugh at himself as he had helped me to "unserious" myself. The three of us said goodnight in a very peaceful mood. Jack went to sleep for the last time.

I sat on the floor the next day, crying and then laughing as Andree and I shared our grief over the phone. Jack and I had released each other long ago. I felt his presence more than ever as did Andree. A friend of mine once told me of a Native American ceremony in which the person who is approaching death lies in the middle of a spiraling circle of tribe members. If the person dies while in the circle, a cheer goes up among those remaining as if the spirit of the deceased has entered everyone assembled. The memorial service would be a party at Jack's request, and I would be bringing the balloons.

The next day, I got a call from Mom in California telling me that Dad had a stroke. He had never really recovered from a quadruple bypass surgery he had previously had. I traveled and that night I was in Riverside, California, and for the next three days Mom and I sat with him. He had decided that he was ready to die. He refused food, water, and medicine. He'd had enough pain and exhaustion. Mom and I, along with the doctors, supported his decision and he was moved into hospice care, which was where we began a most profound conversation. Dad was a devout atheist who had trouble accepting a son devoted to spiritual pursuits, yet there I was—feeling like a "death coach" guiding him through his transition with spiritual tools and without reference to God.

We talked openly about death. He was ready to go and a little impatient about when he would be able to get it over with. Suddenly, we were engaged in a lengthy discussion about religion. He remarked, "I envy people who believe in God. They can turn it over to God and I don't have anyone to turn it over to." Later, as he came out of one of his dreams, I asked him, "Was that Karl Marx or Carl Reiner?" an inside joke of ours. He smiled and quoted an old interview on Johnny Carson: "You can send it to Carl Reiner on Strawberry Fart Lane." We laughed and Dad drifted off again.

At the end of the first day, when Mom and I were leaving, he inquired aloud, "What's the next step?" He had the sense that he was holding on to life and was ready to let it go. I responded,

"Your body goes away and your spirit enters my heart and Mom's heart forever." He liked that idea and—smiling serenely—drifted off to sleep.

The next day, we talked about acceptance, forgiveness, and gratitude being three pathways that made letting go easier. He was doing well on acceptance of his own death. He had always struggled with forgiveness. I reminded him that as Jews, we tended to only practice forgiveness once a year, at Yom Kippur. He chuckled. He was weaker but had many moments of clarity. Sometimes he would just look up, staring a thousand miles out into space. It was as if all of his attention—that magnificent concentration of his—was directed inward, a silent struggle against what felt like a void.

I remember a time many, many years ago when I lived in Atlanta and Dad was at the Musician's Union trying to play hardball politics with the soft heart of an old left-wing liberal. I spoke with him weekly about how to detach from the drama. I was his stress coach, guiding him about how to take the pressure off of himself. I would query, "Are these people willing to die for you?" He'd reply with a decisive "No!" and I'd retort, "Then why are you dying (stressing yourself out) for them?" There I was, twenty years later, holding Dad's hand, kissing his forehead and telling him that I was sorry for any pain I had brought him. I stayed beside him, coaching him through his transition.

On the third day, I went to hospice and the nurses were all running around. I asked what was going on. "Your father wants some chocolate ice cream!" they said, which contradicted his request that he not be fed any food. I am guessing that for him, as for many of us, chocolate ice cream trumps the rules.

That day I spent a lot of time lying in bed with him, holding hands and serenading him with jazz. I stayed late that third night. I had to get back to Memphis the next day and Dad was already essentially unconscious. Within twenty-four hours, he was gone.

⥀⦚⥣⦚⥀

BRIGHT MOMENT: In the days following his death, I found myself telling and retelling the story of those miraculous three days, savoring the intimacy and spiritual bond we shared. This was in attunement with my lifelong spiritual journey of releasing myself from the bonds of convention and remembering I was born naked. We were victorious over years of separation, anger, and disappointment. What remained was love and peace between us.

⥀⦚⥣⦚⥀

I flew out to California on the seventeenth of April for a memorial party. My father had chosen to be cremated and wanted a party in his honor, celebrating his life. Mom had put up publicity pictures of all the big bands Dad had played with—Benny Goodman, Tommy Dorsey, Artie Shaw, and many others. Sixty people were in attendance. Jazz friends, helpful neighbors, relatives—each came with anecdotes to share about Dad. Nothing too formal; just the way Dad would have liked it. Here's to my dad, Sid Weiss, a man of courage and passion—a life worth celebrating. He experienced death as a conscious choice, as a transition. A pioneer in the twenty-first century.

Parents

After my father died, I invited my mother to Memphis from California for a party and a long-needed visit. Everybody loved her. She was sweet, smart, and very funny. A friend of mine and I entertained her with selections from Mel Brooks's 2000-Year-Old Man, which we had memorized.

We had about thirty people at the party, and after a gay and friendly evening, everyone left and my mother and I stood in the kitchen. After a long pause, she said, "Your father was a terrible father. He never knew how to bond with you and your brother." I know she never would have told me that while my father was alive. I knew it was true, and I had done enough therapy over the years that there was little emotional impact for me in her statement. It was more a matter of fact.

I had come to feel some compassion for my father and sorrow for the richness he missed from both me and Gene. We hugged each other and got a good night's sleep. We never spoke of my father's paternal skills again.

After my father's death, my mother had begun to have hallucinations that he was standing at the door to the bedroom. She decided to enter a grief group, in which she immediately became a star. After a few months, the hallucinations went away, and my mother stayed on as a grief coach.

Over the years, I came to learn how to name the various dysfunctions of my family. I occasionally run across a picture of my brother and me, holding hands, and looking innocent. I thought that because of my father's inability to extend himself to me and my brother Gene, we developed a competitiveness that shut us out from emotional connection. Even later in life, when my brother went to prison for possession of sixteen kilos of marijuana, we never wrote to one another.

Perhaps the greatest disappointment I have with myself was my inability to break through that dark distance between us. Even though Gene developed arthritis a year and a half after I did, we never really talked about it. When my friend Ed Puplampu was training me in karate, I had been keeping it a secret, but one day Gene saw us practicing in the backyard. Later that day, after Ed had gone, my brother came into my room saying that, after all of my experience with arthritis, I would never be able to do anything with karate.

I found myself automatically getting into a pose, and as he came closer to me and attempted to kick me, I came down hard on his foot in a way that literally scared him, and he never threatened me again. I never knew the extent of his own pain until later after reading some letters he had sent from the Merchant Marines.

My mother died in 2002, at the age of ninety-two. She had traveled with big bands all over the country. She had lived a very full life, and she knew it. When she was dying, she called me from LA and said to me, "It's time." She'd had enough, so I flew out there to be with her. I took her home and called a hospice nurse to come. It was her time. Maybe this comes when you get older . . . when your body is ready to go, you are ready to go.

We brought her out of the hospital to her home and I sat with her as she prepared to die. At one point she sat bolt upright and said impatiently, "How do you DO this?" I assured her that it was okay for her to leave, and within two hours she passed.

There are some people who are terribly frightened of dying, but my mother wasn't one of those people. She felt that she had put in her time, and she died very peacefully.

World's Largest Balloon Sculpture

I came up with the concept for the World's Largest Balloon Sculpture when I was working as the Religious Education Director for the Unitarian church in Sepulveda, California, in 1965. I had created many of them over the years from California to Georgia and many places in between. It also became the featured event for the Arts Festival of Atlanta's Children's Day for twenty years.

It was featured at the Memphis in May festival where Al Gore, who was in town at the time, asked me if he could participate. And he did. It scared the dickens out of his Secret Service men when the balloon popping stage began.

The World's Largest Balloon Sculpture was designed as a family-oriented, community-participation art experience that puts children and adults in a position of equal power. Everyone who participated in these events would twist together tens of thousands of long, skinny balloons into one gigantic freeform sculpture. It is a wonderful opportunity for adults and children to play together as equals in a magical art event.

The construction process for each of these sculptures would generally last for about eight hours. These events were also devised to raise funds for wonderful and deserving causes. The second balloon sculpture in Memphis was held at the Overton Park Shell on June 5, 2004. The goal of this event was to raise $50,000 for Le Bonheur Children's Medical Center. The spectacle was televised and highly publicized, showing to the world the great variety of cultural groups that made up the city of Memphis.

The guidelines for the building of the World's Largest Balloon Sculpture hadn't changed from the guidelines at its inception: first and foremost, you could not do it wrong! There was no wrong way to do it, and everyone was right. If by some unfortunate chance, someone's balloon popped, they would get an automatic hug. This automatic hug was also optional.

In this activity, the equal status of children and adults create safety and cooperation. When the sculpture was finished, admired, marveled at, photographed, and praised, we would bring it down to the ground.

The first to take action were the young children about three feet tall or shorter who would leap in to stomp the balloons to their hearts' content. Then the taller folk would bring the little ones out and join together to tear it down and stomp it into oblivion.

There was no charge to participate in the balloon sculpture, but donations were welcomed and encouraged, as they would go to help some very worthy causes. Donations would be dropped by or people would, as a contribution, buy one hundred balloons to be inflated and added to the sculpture.

There were many different ways for people of the community to support the creation of the World's Largest Balloon Sculpture other than monetary donations; aside from the actual sculptors, there was a need for people to act in a wide array of supportive duties. With a need for everything from construction crews to safety and cleanup supervisors, food and drink distributors to people who contact businesses about possible donations, there was something to be done for anyone and everyone who wanted to help.

COPENHAGEN

My First Copenhagen Jazz Festival

I had a tradition of going to the Copenhagen Jazz Festival that continued for over thirteen years. I have performed with the Monday Night Big Band, a bunch of jam sessions, and have been a guest at a number of concerts.

While I was living in Memphis, sitting in at Blues Alley and doing occasional concerts with my band, Heaven on Earth, I had gone to a conference in Southern California where I met a guy from Copenhagen named Thor. Thor told me about the great jazz festival that is held there every year and encouraged me to go. My father had told me that there was nothing quite as fine as playing jazz in front of a European audience, so I was sold and began making my travel arrangements.

The following July, I was in Copenhagen. I walked into one of the clubs and asked if I could sit in. They were cordial and invited me onto the stage. The next thing I knew, the audience was yelling and screaming, and I was getting a standing ovation.

Later that evening, I was invited by the same rhythm section to sing at a jam session that started at one o'clock in the morning. The club, La Fontaine, was grimy, noisy, smoky, and smelled of beer. It was just perfect for an after-hours jam session.

For some reason—maybe because I look a bit like an accountant—the place went dead silent as I stepped onto the stage. I sang slowly at first, and then I began to swing. When I started to scat sing, the place went absolutely nuts—more screaming and yelling. I was in heaven.

After that amazing experience, I would try to attend Jazz Festival every summer for as long as my health would allow. When I couldn't make it to Copenhagen because of my health, I would try to find other ways to fill the void. In Memphis, I have been sitting in with a great singer named Joyce Cobb for a weekly Sunday Jazz Brunch since about 2002.

Jazz Festival Foot Infection

I was in Copenhagen for the Jazz festival and had developed an infection in my foot. Since I was apartment-bound, I decided to go inside to experience what I had been learning in Internal Family Systems to open a self-affirming inner dialogue. After all, I had been doing this work with my clients, and it seemed only fair that I do it with myself in this place of joy.

I set up my computer and began to type in a stream of consciousness approach. At first, I felt gratitude to be able to slow down while recuperating. It gave me nourishment to reflect on the adventures I'd had, the many late-night jazz clubs at which I had sung, and the new friends I had made. I was beginning to be recognized by jazz fans and felt very welcome in the clubs.

I was experiencing a deep sense of fulfillment. The group of friends I made loved traveling around the festival with me. Although the arthritis slowed me down, I was full of energy and able to handle my pain levels easily and well. I felt that I was being filled with enough energy and joy to last me until the next Jazz Festival. All of my inner parts were filled with gratitude.

SEEING

What happens when your eyes are open?
    Boom!! You are feeling
       falling
           flying

    pain is
       most certainly
          with you

    Joy is no less
       with you

    Embarrassed blood rushing
       flushing face
          alive
in your guts
       no monotone
          a song

    A creepy crawly curiosity
       that leads you to the
          big-little
             not the middle

    And yet you see,
       looking out,
          the center of your
             me

Log from Copenhagen Jazz Festival 2013

Bear with me as I take you on a tour of the Jazz Festival…

Here We Are Again at The Copenhagen Jazz Festival

This is my seventeenth (1996-2013) year at the festival. The weather is beautiful. Copenhagen is beautiful. Caring friends surround me. I just got a paying gig for Tuesday night with an old and dear friend and guitarist named Tao (pronounced Tay-o) Hojgaard. (He and I played my first paid performance in Copenhagen seventeen years ago.) Even the bass player, Kristor, is here. Here is a poem that captures the feeling of being at the festival:

COPENHAGEN LIGHT

Air is water, water air

The thick glistening streets
Fly up with tenor saxophones
Reaching for the dreamsound
The one that grabs the heart's strings
And tugs you to the bliss
Of divine attention

When it's right, fluid and alive
You stand up on the edge of your hair
For a bright moment, illuminated
Lightened up, enlightened, unsighted

Possessed of powers a thousand engines strong
And you are inside your benediction
Swinging in timeless space

Jazz language groans and sweats
Flights of pansy bright yellow wings
Danish minds tickled until laughter erupts
Knowing smiles that breach the serious within
Clapping in 4/4 delight, audience turning gold
Knowing that without their ears the music is lost

This is the listening we are singing into

The Copenhagen Logs

Friday, July 5, 2013

Deep friends, Lisbeth and her son Lucas gave me the tour of the southern portion of Copenhagen . . . lovely, rich green countryside and farmland with a few castles that dot the area.

Lisbeth, Tina, and I went to see the Mike Stern/Victor Wooten Band. It was like eating the best New York cheesecake. Every sound was rich and filling. They went from the wildest improvisation to the most sublime, sweet, heart-touching music and then to light and playful.

This was the second time I had seen supreme bass virtuoso Victor Wooten in the last two months. He never ceases to amaze me. I love being in the presence of a musician who is playing at such a high level of musicianship that it literally seems impossible.

Guitarist Mike Stern has been around for thirty years. He played with Blood, Sweat & Tears, Miles Davis, and many others. The band featured Bob Franceschini on tenor sax and Derico Watson on drums.

Saturday, July 6, 2013

A relaxing day out in the country at Lisbeth's house. This evening, we went into Copenhagen to meet Tina for dinner and to hear Christina Dahl (sax), Marilyn Mazur (percussion) and Band Ane (computer synthesized music). It was a difficult mix. Lisbeth thinks it was excessive female hormones. Tina hated the computer, and I barely found it tolerable and I'm a tolerant guy. Lisbeth says the bar had a nice ginger ale . . . ah well.

Jazz at its best is experimental and at its most difficult it's experimental. Christina and Marilyn together make beautiful music. The impression I had was that the synthesized music had difficulty integrating into them. The integration is still immature.

Sunday July 7, 2013

It's a fabulous, mild, sunny day at Kongens Have (king's garden). Two thousand people are hanging out in the park listening to the A-Team, the cream of the crop of mainstream jazz musicians led by Niels Jorgen Steen. Lots of great Basie and Neil Hefti Arrangements. The singer, Bobo Moreno, has real mastery on Sinatra-style phrasing and the solos were smooth and swinging.

My then-fiancé Sherry and I had stayed at his apartment ten festivals ago and he and his friend Mette-Marie had visited me in Memphis around that time.

After the concert, we went to an organic restaurant for dinner and then to a fantastic blues concert performed by Poul Banks (guitar and vocals), Hugo Rasmussen (bass), Martin Anderson (violin) and Jorgen Lang (vocals, harmonica). These guys have been playing together for over thirty years and they are really tight. They blend some Southern blues, a little country and create a great mixture of sincere poignancy and humor. I found myself laughing out loud at their subtle musical humor. These guys have lived life deeply and convey it in their tone and the way they communicate with one another and the audience. We left fulfilled.

Monday, July 8, 2013

I am getting very excited. I will be performing six times with great musicians during the festival.

Later that night, with my own Memphis arrangement by Carl Wolf, I sang "Joy Spring" with the Monday Night Big Band at a festival club, and I nailed it!!! These musicians are unsurpassed. It has become one of my own greatest joys over the years to have Nils Jorgen Steen consider me "a tradition" and invite me yearly to performing with this talented band.

Tomorrow night I have a full gig with my friend and excellent guitarist Tao Hoejgaard. Seventeen years ago, we did our first gig together. In those days his hair was extremely short and on the top of his head was tattooed a large yin-yang symbol.

Lisbeth, Tina, and I went to the Carlsberg concert area to hear a tribute to Art Blakey, one of the founders of the type of jazz known as bebop. Almost every great horn player and piano player that became famous in New York played in Blakey's band, The Jazz Messengers.

The band at Carlsberg was led by Krestin Osgood, a wonderful drummer who has played with some of the world's greatest musicians. The concert was comprised of many obscure recordings by the Art Blakey band, many of them very difficult. We ate from their tasty smorgasbord, sat in the sun and relaxed to the music. One particular tune, "Contemplation," written by Wayne Shorter, was exquisitely melodic and peaceful.

Tuesday, July 9, 2013

Tuesday evening: Club Bo-Bi (pronounced booby). I thought my friends would think I was pole dancing. It was a full evening of jazz with Tao Hoejgaard on guitar and Kristor Brodgaard on bass. Over the last seventeen years, I have sung on the same stage with them. It was a small intimate club with a very attentive audience.

Before the gig, I had sent Tao a list of tunes that we could do together. He seemed reluctant about some of the tunes (old jazz standards). I took it to mean that he probably thought I was an old fogy and he wanted to play more avant-garde tunes. Toward the end of the gig, however, he revealed to me that in such small quarters, he didn't want to have to read the music. So, I guess I'm not a musical dinosaur. Hooray!

Wednesday, July 10, 2013

We have been calling today "Nette day" because Lisbeth and I are going to have dinner with an old friend who is leaving for Spain tomorrow.

Later that night: dinner with Nette was fun at a restaurant with a jump band (one that plays lots of upbeat swing and blues tunes.) Nette is an old Copenhagen friend who is smart and gentle with very clear energy.

After dinner we went to the Blue Dog, a spacious and well-appointed jazz club, to hear a wonderful jazz singer named Katrine Madsen. All I can say is "wowie zowie." I have seen her a couple of times but never in such fine form. The place was packed, and Katrine had the room totally in her hands. Her voice was serene. She showed an incredible range and a knack for the playful. The three of us fell under her spell, as did everyone else.

Thursday, July 11, 2013

Today was a big day. Every year I attend the jazz brunch and jam session at the beautiful Kong Arthur Hotel. The courtyard was packed with musicians who were honored by the event.

Here's the scene: warm friendly people, blue sky, comfortable chairs, and the smell of genuine jambalaya and hors d'oeuvres. Ahhhh, the clinking sound of bottles of wine and beer . . . all of it free and delicious. There is a great jazz quartet playing. Mrs. Brochner and her mother, owners of the Kong Arthur Hotel, warmly welcomed me back.

On the way to the Kong Arthur, I was remembering that last year I was introduced to a wonderful couple, Ellen Bick

Assmusen and Svend Assmusen. Svend played jazz violin all over the world and is very popular in Denmark. His wife is a talented and charming writer.

As Lisbeth and I drove to the Kong Arthur it came into my mind that we would sit next to the Asmussens and, lo and behold, we arrived and there were empty seats next to the Asmussens and in front of the band. For the rest of the afternoon, in between performances, we engaged in the most uplifting conversation imaginable. Ellen is a transplant from New York who fell in love with the Scandinavian landscape, language, and ultimately with Svend.

They are both discriminating lovers of jazz. Svend is a mere ninety-seven (and a half). He had a stroke a few years ago but maintains a strong memory and his love for and knowledge of music is clearly a tonic for him and for Ellen. Her love for Svend is evident in every move she makes with him. Her message to Lisbeth and me was, "It's never too late. Love has not abandoned you."

She pulled out two copies of her book of poetry with some of Svend's written music. It is called Scandinavian Solstice (publisher: Lindhardt and Ringhof). I have only just begun to read it and am struck by the lean poetic lines, so much like the Danish landscape and the clarity and loving dedication Ellen and Svend have for each other. What a gift to meet them and, as it were, to receive their blessing.

The place was crawling with outstanding musicians and singers. When I saw an opening, I sang "Stella by Starlight" and was enthusiastically received. This place is like home to me. After hours of great music, good food, inspiring conversation, and a beautiful day in the sun, we took our leave.

After I sang, Svend told Ellen that he thought I was very musical. I took that as a supreme compliment coming from Svend.

At Lisbeth's suggestion, we drove back to Koge to a restaurant overlooking the sea with an outstanding seafood buffet, with lobster, oysters, tuna, mussels, etc. It was a two-and-a-half-hour feast. Stuffed, full of fabulous memories, food, music, and inspirational fellowship, we slept like babies.

Friday, July 12, 2013

What a day! Tina, Lisbeth and I met at Carlsberg to hear a tribute to Cannonball Adderly, one of the world's most prodigious and uplifting alto sax players. Years ago, I saw him in Fresno, California with Miles Davis and John Coltrane. It was one of the greatest and most innovative bands ever. The music they wrote and performed is still influential today.

I was a little disappointed at this band's instrumentation (The Jesper Lundgaard Trio). I was expecting a larger group to capture Cannonball's bigger sound. There were some old hits, in particular, Bobby Timmons's "Work Song." I couldn't help but sing along.

And now, imagine: Tina, Lisbeth, and I are walking through Christiania, a free state in the middle of Copenhagen. Approximately half a century ago when the Danish navy was decommissioned, hippies and other free thinkers and stone-heads occupied the empty buildings. To this day Christiania is a community with benefits. That is, if you want to score some marijuana or hashish, or fresh bread, or jewelry, or 1960's style clothes, or nice food, this is the place to go.

It is almost 10 pm and we are ascending the stairs at the Loppen (which means "the flea") where I am performing. The room is dark, the bathroom is male/female and there is enough power in the speakers and amplifiers to level a small village.

I have been invited by my guitarist friend Tao to perform what he calls DJazz. It is a combination of DJ, hip hop music, rap, jazz, and a new addition . . . me doing spoken word.

I came a long distance from a frankly snobbish, purist, be-bop jazz mindset, where you know your musical parameters and you push them as you get better. This time I have no idea where we are headed, nor does Tao. We know we are going to do it and we know who the players are.

Before we get started my mind starts to race with clever inner repartee. I share some bright ideas with Tao and he puts his hand comfortingly on my shoulder and says, "Let it flow. We'll make room for you." I relaxed immediately.

Tao had his guitar running through a complex synthesizer that was part science fiction soundtrack and part rhythm box. The bass player, Kristor, had his own synthesized sound and DJ Scratch Majic played a mix of synthesized sound and extremely sophisticated vinyl record manipulation.

My rules for the gig were for me not to sing or to talk about jazz . . . just spoken word. I laid back until the music settled in and then I started talking about the mother of rhythm being the heartbeat or our footsteps and from there I have no idea where I headed. But it was good.

We got into a groove and stayed there. The more I relaxed, the more room there was for me. After the first tune (I don't really think "tune" fits, but I had already run out of descriptive vocabulary), Tao introduced a young rapper named Agami who was startling, smart, and creative. Tao encouraged us to have a spontaneous conversation while the band played "space music." I would have to watch the videotape to know what happened, but I do remember "tell the truth, tell the truth . . ."

Sometime toward the end of the first set, the bass player kicked in at a volume level that felt like it was going to turn my ribs to jelly. I expected Tina and Lisbeth to be begging to get out of there and, instead, they were excited and wanted more.

Into the second set we flew. After some more space music, Tao asked me to perform an eco-blues I wrote based on a drone sound. What was usually a five-minute piece turned into at least twenty minutes with Tao doing some incredible improvising.

At the end of the set, I was really exhilarated. I had expanded my concept of jazz to include elements I never imagined I would. Lisbeth and Tina told me I was moving with the music as if I were dancing in space.

Saturday, July 13, 2013

Another gorgeous day. Tina, Lisbeth, and I arrived back at Carlsberg to hear a tribute to Oscar Pettiford, a well-known bop bass player who died in Copenhagen a number of years ago. Hugo Rasmussen led the band on bass. He knew Oscar Pettiford (back in the days of Thelonious Monk, Oscar was called O.P.).

In the second set, Hugo asked me to come on stage and perform "Stella by Starlight." I was feeling very powerful, and my voice sounded like it. Toward the end of the tune, I motioned to Hugo for us to trade fours (improvise alternating four-bar passages, like a conversation). I sang a bass part, and he played one. What great fun. The audience loved it.

Later that night, Lisbeth and I went back to hear more of Katrine Madsen. Pure inspiring luxury.

Sunday, July 14, 2013

Ah! The last day of the festival. Also, a day for packing and moving from Lisbeth's and her son Lucas' house to Tina's house. Everything moved smoothly. Lisbeth, Lucas, Tina, and Lisbeth's friend Annette arrived at the scene of the closing concert of the festival. We were at Islands Brygge on the water, looking at the city.

The band was led by Hugo Rasmussen All Starz. We had a wonderful buffet and settled in for some great classic swing and bebop.

Hugo asked me onto the stage in the middle of the second set. I sang "There'll Never be Another You" and was accompanied by Hugo; Krestin Osgood, a world class drummer; and Christina von Bulow, a great talented alto sax player. I had wanted to perform with Christina for years.

After I took three choruses, she and a great tenor sax player named Jacob Dineson performed jazz solos simultaneously driving the audience wild. I was in heaven.

After another tune, a young bass player from an island near Copenhagen performed with Hugo as a duet and they generated immense intensity. The band and the audience were thrilled.

One touching moment occurred when the young bassist soloed and everyone on stage was transfixed, listening with great care and nodding as his creativity shone through.

The night was complete, and I could not have been more fulfilled with this magnificent climax to a fabulous, creative, energized Copenhagen Jazz Festival. As Hugo said, "Same time next year."

Over the years I have been struck by the outstanding architecture in Copenhagen and, on this trip, also in Malmo, Sweden. Tina and I took a day trip across the bridge to Malmo. We were struck by a building labeled "The Turning Torso." It is fifty-five stories and houses businesses and apartment condominiums. We weren't able to take a tour, but just being close to it was pretty stunning.

The Turning Torso in Malmo, Sweden. Look it up.

Thank you for indulging me down memory lane.

BACK IN MEMPHIS

Nancy, Coffee?

Dr. Jameson's examination room is cramped. I have come for a second opinion on my arthritic feet, and as I suspected, he is telling me that there is no surgical answer. But he can put orthotics in my shoes that will diminish the pain.

His nurse checks my blood pressure, and seeing that it is quite balanced, she asks, "What's your secret?" I look at her and say, "I'm mellow." She is laughing and looks at my medication list and sees that I am taking Wellbutrin, a common antidepressant, and says, "Here's your mellow. I take the same medication."

I ask her how long she's been working at OrthoMemphis. "Twenty-eight years," she tells me. I reply, "That's real commitment." As she was leaving the room, she turned with a smile on her face and stated, "I can handle commitment." That was a trigger.

Walking down the hall toward the X-ray room, I see her again and the smiles between us are full of energy. I'm feeling led to connect with her and find myself pulling my business card out and writing on the back my cell phone number and the words, "Nancy, coffee?"

As I am walking past her desk, I notice a colorful ring on her ring finger, and suspect that she's married. I feel a thud in my heart. Oh my God, I am ten years too late.

A line from a movie I'd just seen called We Bought a Zoo with Matt Damon pops into my mind. In the movie, his brother says to him, "All you need is twenty seconds of courage." I am breathing deeply. "Are you married?" She says, "My husband died a year and a half ago." As if choreographed, my hand reaches out and hands her my card. She reads it and laughs, saying, "I'd like that! I'll call you." As I leave OrthoMemphis, I feel as though my life is being guided gently and now all I have to do is wait.

Early in the evening, I am receiving my first text in months. At the same moment, Nancy is pacing back and forth in her bedroom, her three dogs sitting on the bed, their heads following her in unison, back and forth, back and forth. Finally, I am receiving a text that says, "I think you are intelligent and funny—two qualities I admire. I'll call you for coffee." Immediately, another text shows up that says, "Also, I think you're a smart ass—another quality I admire." It feels like my heart is being pried open.

Almost everything that followed our first meeting was easy.

I quickly realized that Nancy was my teacher. Her gentleness and warmth and sincerity made everything rich. My heart can't believe its good luck. At the age of seventy-two, I was completely in love.

I met Nancy in late September, and on Thanksgiving Day of that same year, I asked her to marry me.

HEARTS CAN JOIN

Permission is given in red tulip spring
open doors wide
to love and dance
slippery as laughter

hearts can join

Permission is given in balloon crazy spring
loosen your belt
breathe life and leap
friendly is catching
hearts can join

Permission is given in brer rabbit spring
touching is easy
to smile and to bathe
clever as midnight
hearts can join

Permission is given in I love you spring
feel the sky rise
your hand my hand
mistletoe year 'round
hearts can join

Permission is given in I choose you spring
open your you
and let me jump in
lovingly tender touch
hearts can join

❧ ✠ ☙

The wedding was a joyful hippie wedding. We had the ceremony in the park in spring with a great band and surrounded by loved ones. The event was comprised of musician friends, family members, a small balloon sculpture, a potluck dinner, and my godson, Jamel, playing tenor sax.

People visiting the park mistook our joyful event for the Memphis in May celebration and crashed it, which was totally fine! A wonderful finale came as Nancy was walking toward the wedding gazebo. She reached into her flowers and pulled out a kazoo. She began to play the Wedding March. Everyone that was there pulled out their own kazoo and provided a kazoo choir, playing the Wedding March.

In the years since that time, Nancy and I have grown closer every day. Since then, we have travelled to Copenhagen twice for the Jazz Festival, to Cancun twice, staying at a million-dollar castle on the ocean, and several trips to see our families. We have also faced several health issues together, and almost always come away laughing about it. Despite all the ailments that come along with growing older, I feel very secure and happy with Nancy by my side.

At last!

Bar Talk at Bosco's

Bosco's Restaurant and Brewing Company in midtown Memphis has been the venue for Joyce Cobb and her band for decades and a musical home for me, Dr. Scat, for most of those years. We always have a wonderful time.

I play games in my head. In my experience of singing at predominantly white clubs, I've concocted an imaginary character who has a pointed inner question which sounds something like this: "What the HEYELL is he doin'?! Did he forgit the goddam words?!"

I AM 53 YEARS OF ROMPIN' STOMPIN' LIFE

There is an awakening
    Beyond Age
        Or even death

Looking in is not looking back
    It is looking into the light

I am 53 years of rompin', stompin' life
    I sing you my birthday
        And the years to come

Here, swimming in a sea of hearts
    Sliding through mind trips
        I must have made up

I am most in love when I sing
    Most at home
        My mind free of words
Into pure total bliss
    I careen from chord to chord
        The ride of my life
Every song a chance to break free

I want to take you with me
    Away or above or through
        The word world

Step aboard the 53rd edition of me

The year of singing cougar,
Hugananda
Captain Video
The Balloon Sculptor
Dr. Love
Dr. Scat

⁓✺⁓

After the gig, Joyce, the band, and I would gather at the bar and philosophize about the sorry state of America's decline and who or what was to "blame."

Education—or the lack thereof—was proclaimed, economics, the unfairness of it all. The inevitable racism. The astronomical cost of health care and on and so forth.

As the invisible talking stick came to me, "Consciousness," I said. There was a barely noticeable tiny pause. A poof! A vacuum and a large nothing. The talking stick moved on and I shrugged.

Naked Again

The major threads of my life have been exploring consciousness and the heart-mind connection, innovative therapies, courage and fearlessness, commitment to social empowerment, championing the underdog, standing naked and real and all that means (which actually means the willingness to reveal myself to the core), belief in the power of joy, stepping into life as a commitment and a surprise, living in a state of wonder with the eyes and heart of a child, and music—especially jazz.

The defining feature of jazz is surprise. Improvisation is a high-wire act. You have to both balance and allow yourself to be off-balance. It is a community expression created in concert with unique individuals. Life is improvisation. We think we have it all organized but we are all improvising. I have learned to treasure the bright moments of improvisation that I have shared with you. It is the naked truth of a loving heart.

Now in my mid-eighties, I am still riding the pony of life, hanging on to creative energy. I have learned to be more kind and forgiving of myself for the silly assumptions and allegations I make about the chaos of life. Perhaps the Universe is testing my sense of humor.

Writing this book has been an emotional roller-coaster. The allegory of seeing a mirror for the first time changes everything.

Thank you for walking beside me in this act of self-discovery.

❦

ME AT 83

I am no longer The Hub
Bringer of the spark
No longer A hub

83 moments
In a more subtle, dimming light
Once full to bright

Now heeding the road sign
On my walker
Saying "don't Fall!"

Still able to chuckle
At the mask of silly pretense

Stuffed full of rich Dreams
Delicious stored in lustrous leather luggage

Musical chairs
No longer quick enough
to land with any certainty at all

With a liberating hopelessness
Joyful breathing,

Free.

Acknowledgement Page

The woman who kept me alive throughout the writing of this book my wife Nancy. Her patience born of having been a nurse for fifty years and her devotion to keeping my life organized and safe. To whom I'm eternally grateful.

To Jocelyn Regenwether, who devotedly encouraged me taking hours and hours of my sometime halting dictation. A true friend and teacher.

To Elaine Orland, a voluntary witness to my stories, To whom I'm forever indebted and whose editing assistance often bought us both to tears and uproarious laughter. I cannot thank you enough.

To Elaine's husband David, for his precise and clear copyediting.

To the rich and amazing cast of characters that populate the book, all of them my teachers, I live in gratitude.

www.ingramcontent.com/pod-product-compliance
Lightning Source LLC
Chambersburg PA
CBHW071214090426
42736CB00014B/2812